Bothered by Alligators

Milner's final text, *Bothered by Alligators*, came about when, in her nineties, she unexpectedly came across a diary she had kept during the early years of her son's life, recording his conversations and play between the ages of 2 and 9. With it was a story book written and illustrated by him when he was about 7 years old.

Whilst working on the material, Milner gradually realised that both diary and story book were provoking questions she realised had scarcely been asked, let alone answered, in her own analysis. Through her memories, her notebooks and by interpreting her own previously discarded drawings and paintings, she reaches a point of awareness that they were depicting things she did not know in herself, addressing her relationships not only with her son but also with her husband, her father and, in particular, her mother.

Like many of Milner's earlier books there is a deeply personal quality to *Bothered by Alligators,* but it is a quality that transcends the personal and reveals insights and conclusions that will be both interesting and useful to clinicians; and fascinating to readers from a psychological, a literary, an artistic or an educational background, and, in particular, those with an interest in psychoanalysis and autobiography and in Milner's work.

Marion Milner (1900–1998) was a distinguished British psychoanalyst, educationalist, autobiographer and artist.

Margaret Walters spent many years as a university lecturer, broadcaster and writer. She was a longstanding friend of Marion Milner and, at Marion's request, became her Literary Executor after her death.

Emma Letley is a writer, academic and psychoanalytic psychotherapist, trained with the Arbours Association, and practising in Notting Hill Gate and at King's College London. She is the biographer of Marion Milner.

Photo of John as a young boy

Bothered by Alligators

Marion Milner

Introduction by Margaret Walters

Series Editor: Emma Letley

Literary Executors: John Milner and Margaret Walters

Routledge
Taylor & Francis Group

LONDON AND NEW YORK

First published 2012
by Routledge
2 Park Square, Milton Park, Abingdon, Oxfordshire, OX14 4RN

Simultaneously published in the USA and Canada
by Routledge
711 Third Avenue, New York NY 10017

Routledge is an imprint of the Taylor & Francis Group, an Informa business

British Library Cataloguing in Publication Data
A catalogue record for this book is available from the British Library

Library of Congress Cataloging-in-Publication Data
Milner, Marion Blackett.
  Bothered by alligators / Marion Milner ; introduction by Margaret
Walters.
    p. cm.
1. Milner, Marion Blackett—Psychology. 2. Milner, Marion Blackett—
Family. 3. Child psychology. 4. Psychoanalysis. I. Title.
BF109.M55A3 2012
150.92—dc23
[B]

2011027124

ISBN: 978-0-415-68455-2 (hbk)
ISBN: 978-0-415-68456-9(pbk)
ISBN: 978-0-203-14014-7 (ebk)

Typeset in New Century Schoolbook
by RefineCatch Limited, Bungay, Suffolk
Paperback cover design by Andrew Ward

Contents

Illustrations

New Introduction

Margaret Walters

As she writes in her own introduction to *Bothered by Alligators*, Marion Milner began this last book of hers some time in 1990, when she turned 90 herself, after deciding that "it was time, belatedly, to try to get some sort of order into my papers." Typically, she adds, "so as to be ready for being dead, whenever that might be."

These last years were happy, and productive. No matter how bitter the weather, she turned up every Saturday morning at the psychotherapist Nina Farhi's house in north London for meetings of the Squiggle Society, the group devoted to the work of the analyst D.W. Winnicott, whom Marion had known well. (Indeed, one of the last chapters in this book is about her not altogether satisfactory analysis with Winnicott.) But the lively, free-wheeling Squiggle discussions often moved beyond his work to other subjects. Most of the regulars were therapists and analysts, who knew Marion and her writings very well. But there were several outsiders, who were made welcome – and expected to contribute. One of the most respected art dealers in London, Frederick Mulder,[1] was a regular. He led one meeting, showing us Old Master prints from his current stock, discussing them with us, even allowing us to hold them and look at them closely. Marion, with her love of the visual arts, particularly enjoyed that session. After I had been attending there for a few months, I too was asked to contribute. As it was close to Christmas, I did a slide-show of images of the Madonna that ranged from the formally magnificent to the tenderly human, to tragic images of the young mother, foreseeing his destiny, looking down at a baby lying dead in her arms. Marion had interesting things to say about those as well.

Like Adam Philips, who describes regularly going to see her, when they would talk together over a glass of whisky,[2] I often visited her at around six on Wednesdays, when we would drink, and talk, sometimes very seriously, sometimes just gossiping. She was always good company. One of her happiest days in those last years was spent at Imperial College in London, where a bust was unveiled honouring her brother Patrick, the Nobel prize-winning physicist who had been ennobled as Lord Blackett. The two had been very close when they were young; inevitably perhaps, they were less intimate as adults. Marion was quiet, even a little anxious, in the taxi going there. But she blossomed once we arrived. After the formal ceremony and speeches were done, she flitted happily around the crowded hall, telling complete strangers, "That's my brother. He split the atom, you know." Needless to say, everyone seemed both moved and delighted to talk with her.

Marion had been drawing and painting since her teens; one very early painting has survived: a small but rather beautiful image of a peaceful harbour, with a note on the back, saying "painted just after the end of WWI as a celebration." She went on drawing and painting for most of her life.

One of her own favourite works was a large and very striking canvas which hung in her front room, with two red hens aggressively confronting each other. Showing the painting to visitors, she liked to remark, mischievously, that it was an image of Anna Freud and Melanie Klein arguing over who had contributed most to psychoanalysis. Anyone who failed to laugh, or at least look amused, had some ground to make up.

In her later years, in an extraordinary act of creative destruction, Marion cut up many of her canvases and reassembled the pieces to make the abstract, and very beautiful, collages that may prove her most lasting, and are certainly her most distinctive, works of art. Several of the later chapters of *Bothered by Alligators* deal with some of these collages.

Marion was rarely lonely in those last years, although one might speculate that her collages deal with the subject of loneliness and the need for connectedness. But she was close to her son, John, to her grandchildren, and to her many friends. After she died in 1998, we arranged a meeting in her memory, and a series of speakers discussed her work and paid tribute to her contribution to psychoanalysis. One scheduled speaker failed to turn up, and that proved a blessing in disguise. I was chairing the meeting, and on impulse, and a shade nervously, asked if anyone from the audience would like to come up and speak. Dozens of people immediately, and eagerly, took up the offer, and spoke knowledgeably, affectionately, and very movingly, about her: old friends, neighbours, fellow analysts, former patients, people who had met her, however briefly, and many others who knew her through her books and had been beguiled and often deeply moved by them.

Bothered by Alligators was begun when Marion, struggling – at the age of 90 – to sort out her rather chaotic papers, unexpectedly came across a diary she had kept years earlier and almost forgotten, which records her small son's questions, anxieties and games, from the age of 2 until he was about 9. There was also a story book with pictures which the boy – her son John, referred to as "J" in her diary – had made at school, and given to her. On the second page, the child writes "Published March 1939." She admits, sadly, that she had hardly noticed it at the time; that it was only fifty years later that the little boy's gift was recognised and appreciated. His story book and the diary she kept through much of his childhood are the basis of this last book. She showed a draft, somewhat nervously, to friends and colleagues, who assured her that it should indeed be published.

Sorting through her papers, I found an unsigned note, obviously from an old friend, who had seen an early version of the book and remarked, "your writing is always personal, Marion, but this is autobiographical." It is an illuminating comment. *Bothered by Alligators* is clearly not a formal autobiography, but it certainly deals with the details of her own life in a frank and very direct way. She writes about her own parents, about her meeting with, and her marriage in 1927 to, Dennis Milner; about their trip to the United States, and the birth, in 1932, of her only child, John. It was after his early morning feed that she began writing the book that eventually became *A Life of One's Own*, which was published under the name Joanna Field. Marion said she needed a pseudonym in case the book disturbed the teachers at the school where she was working. I once asked her why she chose that particular pseudonym; she laughed and said, "Well, it's a pretty name, and it reminds me of the country."

The title *Bothered by Alligators* came to her when she heard her small son saying softly to himself, "Poor Sara, are the alligators bothering you?" She admits that she was puzzled. Sara was the first name of the charlady who worked for them in London, and came with them on country holidays; her son was devoted to her. In fact, she recalls, the family always called the woman simply "Taylor." But with her ear for the striking phrase, she could not resist the child's words, and used them as the title.

At the age of 90 when Marion really looked at John's story book, she was, however belatedly, deeply moved by it. In this last book, she says, she hoped to show parents how a child "can struggle with the interplay of his own and his parents' problems, and how he can do this by using his poetic intuition long before he can express the problems in direct logical speech." She had moments of anxiety: was she trying to analyse her own son? But she suddenly thought, "No, it's his images analysing me, helping me to find out what had been left out of my own couch analysis."

The story book is colourful, and its stories are many and various. It certainly begins rather grimly, with a tale about a cock killed by a fox, which is then killed by a farmer, who sets traps in which eight foxes and eight rabbits are killed. Another story is about a "grumpy old woman who threw stones at lots of people." But these are followed by a series of short tales and pictures where the characters unusually manage to find "comfort." The word echoes through story after story, longingly perhaps: a little boy lives in the woods in "a very comfortable house"; another boy lives in a hollow tree which is "nice and comfortable and warm"; a fox moves to a new "comfortable home." A kitten whose mother was dead lived "in a very comfortable house."

Several of the characters are described as having fun: a boy living in a caravan thought that it was "great fun to make a hut in the ditch" when it stopped. A boy called Twink lives on a boat, plays dominoes with the lighthouse keeper, and has games on the lighthouse stairs with a dog called Bobby.

It might be thought that the story book, with its alternating of imagery about comfort – the frequent recurrence of house imagery, on the one hand, and on the other an adventurous interest in travel, in trains and boats – reflects any young boy's dichotomy between a desire for security that emanates from his mother, and a need to venture out into the big bad world, the impulse that derives from his father, the person of action. Although he cannot remember much about making the story book so many years later, John himself remarked to me that life at the time he made the story book was "difficult," with his father frequently being away from home, so it is not surprising that the predominant tone in many of his stories is one of unease, and a yearning for that "comfortable" home.

The story book is preceded by Marion's diary (beginning with an undated entry noting that "J was 2") which spans the years from the beginning of 1934 to 1942. For the most part, it records simply and perceptively (without rushing to interpret or analyse) the small boy's chatter and comments, his fantasies and fears, the games he likes to play, the questions he is beginning to ask, his need for her approval of his activities, and his occasional outbursts of anger and frustration. She notes, but seems curiously undisturbed by, the child's anxious concern about his mother's absence, when, in the winter of 1936, she went to Spain, partly because of strains in her marriage, partly because she was looking for the peace and quiet she felt she needed to finish her next book, *An Experiment in Leisure*, which was published in 1937. Her son sent her a picture letter while she was away; she admits, rather sadly, that she had failed to respond to his drawings, completely missing the anger and distress expressed in some of them, thinking them "just scribbles, totally unrecognisable as what J said they were."

This encouraged her to return to the story book, and to try to explore its meaning. Her own attempts to analyse John's story book are complex, and form the core of *Bothered by Alligators*. Not unnaturally, they draw upon her psychoanalytic background, and are concerned with the relationship between the child and the world as expressed in his imagery, and, of course, the relationship between child, mother and father. Much of her interpretation focuses upon J's own body image, his prepubescent sexuality, and that all important relationship with his parents. She notes the frequent appearance of the Oedipus Complex, manifest in his "desire to lie on top of me," and his drawings of men without arms, which, she wonders, perhaps symbolise his "guilt about ideas of attacking his father as a rival, combined with the phallic enjoyment of his own body."

She never quite comes to a definite summation of her son's image-text, but keeps returning to it, teasing out more meanings from it, and using it as a springboard for musings about herself and the relationship with her own mother. Clearly, her own interpretations of the darker portions of the story book and J's dreams lead her to speculate whether the story of the kitten whose mother was dead could have been due, "not only to my many absences and the angry ideas expressed in the 'wrecked train' and the 'terrible dragon' of his picture letter, when surely he could have felt that he had killed me in his imagination."

But despite its troubling aspects, Marion appreciated the opportunity the book gave her for interpreting imagery at a deep level, as she had done in previously published works such as *On Not Being Able to Paint* (1950) and *The Hands of the Living God* (1969). It also demonstrates her evident mother's pride in her son's achievement in making something so creative and complex at such an early age:

I now saw J's book as not only showing all the work that had been done by both his teachers and by himself, learning such things as the shapes of the sounds of the

alphabet and how to write them, also how words are
spelt and the right grammatical order if they are to make
sense. It also shows his capacity both to create and play
with images of his own experience, including images for
his feelings, conflicts, fears and enjoyment, all embodied
in the stories he told himself, the story-telling in fact a
loving gift of himself made by the integrating of work
and play, the love shown in the care taken to produce
what is obviously meant to be read, with its carefully
numbered pages and beautifully painted cover.

Bothered by Alligators is by its nature a fragmentary book.
It was after all written by someone in her nineties, albeit
a remarkable nonagenarian. Much more so than in many
writers, Marion's writing has the precious quality of someone
simply thinking aloud, and it follows where those thoughts
go, sometimes without quite ordering where that might lead
us. That is its charm, but occasionally also its frustration.

   Marion's books can be considered broadly to fall into
two main categories. The first, as we see in the initial and
primary part of *Bothered by Alligators*, is concerned with the
act and experience of making a diary, and then analysing it,
an analysis that, although informed by psychoanalysis, is
far from conventional psychoanalytical theory. Indeed her
first book, *A Life of One's Own* (1934), was inspired by her
decision to keep a diary, after reading Montaigne's *Essays*.
An Experiment in Leisure, written in 1937, also focused
upon the autobiographical process of diary-keeping, as did
Eternity's Sunrise, which has the sub-title *A Way of Keeping
a Diary*, which she wrote in 1987, and is the book which
is perhaps closest to *Bothered by Alligators* in concept.
Although, that said, each of her books is so individualistic and
so conjured from empirical observation and first principles
that comparisons between them are not only invidious but
somewhat futile. Nevertheless, in his fine introduction
to the new edition of *Eternity's Sunrise*, Hugh Haughton
suggests that *A Life of One's Own*, *An Experiment in Leisure*
and *Eternity's Sunrise* can be considered as a loose trio, as
an "experimental autobiographical trilogy written under
the sign of self-analysis."[3] One might now speculate that,

with the addition of *Bothered by Alligators*, the trilogy has become a quartet, except that the other strain in Marion's writing also features here in a crucial and central role.

The second category in Marion's writings (if one can put it like that, for the two aspects are clearly two sides of the same complex coin) deals with the visual arts, primarily the act of making marks – which can be as basic as her friend D.W. Winnicott's "squiggles," or as profound as some of the great religious paintings that she loved. Following the Winnicott tradition, one in which she played her part, she considers this mark-making as not just a form of extrovert self-expression, but a rather more introspective self-exploration – another kind of analysis. *On Not Being Able to Paint* was an investigation into the meaning of her own "free association" paintings, and *The Hands of the Living God*, as Houghton suggests, was a "portrait-cum-case-history built around interpretations of the drawings of a schizophrenic patient she calls Susan." Here, in *Alligators*, her paintings have become collages, since, having become frustrated that she was not "able to paint" because of the physical vicissitudes of old age, she cut up some of her paintings and made new works, cut-and-pasted out of the fragments, rather like Henri Matisse and the cut-out paper "paintings" he made when old age made it impossible for him to paint in the conventional way. Marion discusses some of her own remarkable late works towards the end of *Alligators*, and of course, she had the found imagery of a "patient" to hand in her son's story book – except that her relationship with the maker of these pictures was bound much more closely to her psyche than that with any patient she would deal with in a professional capacity.

In Chapter 7 of *Alligators*, she describes in detail how the collages – which were very important to her - came into being. She cut up paintings that she felt were failures, and played with the pieces, "just shifting them around until some sort of intriguing pattern emerged, which I would then paste up to make a collage." But she set herself a rule: that they should not be abstract, but rather "represent some sort of human (or animal) encounter, although the background could be abstract." She moves on to an intriguing and thought-provoking discussion of a collage that she called, inspired by a Walter de la Mare poem, *The Listeners*, which she "had always loved, but never felt I had understood." It is certainly a powerful, even disturbing piece of writing, with its Traveller knocking at a moonlit door, heard only by a "host of phantom listeners." Marion admits that she is still uncertain about just what it is saying, though she wonders if it could be a poem "about madness, about retreat from the world of men." But looking at the same collage later, she caught a "hovering memory" of another poem that seemed to be totally in contrast to the mood of the de la Mare one, but which now seemed to speak to her – George Herbert's *The Banquet* [Love (III)] ("Love bade me welcome: yet my soul drew back Guilty of dust and sin..."). She goes on to write – always in a self-questioning, exploratory, sometimes free-associating way – about some of her other collages – one which "called itself 'The Green Baby'," another which "called itself 'Woebegone'."

She also returns to images that were in John's story book, explaining that though she could analyse what his pictures "might be saying for him, I did not really know how to use this for myself." So she found herself relating them to her own images, which in her earlier writing she had termed "beads." And the final part of the book shifts away from her relationship with her son, back into the past, into an exploration of her memories of her own parents. Her last few chapters are more straightforwardly autobiographical. "I now felt the need to write more about my father," she begins, and her very real affection for him is shadowed by anxiety about a bad fall he had, as well as her concern that for a time at least he seemed so confused. But in 1917, the family inherited some money, moving from Guildford to the country, where her father for his war work became the village postman. "He enjoyed all this greatly," she recalls. And she prints out his last affectionate letter to her, written not long before he died.

Her memories of her mother are perhaps more disturbing; she slowly came to see that her mother might have been "secretly unhappy in her marriage," disillusioned perhaps, and towards the end of her mother's life, they became much closer. Some of her happiest memories are of her brother. At first, she had envied him because he was not expected to help with housework; but on what she recalls as a memorable day, the pair "discovered each other in playing together." And she recalls, very movingly, her last memory of him (by now a Nobel prize winner, a Companion of Honour, and Life Peer, Baron Blackett of Chelsea) dying in the Middlesex Hospital in 1974.

The final section of the book sees Marion moving from subject to subject, memory to memory, evoking those "spots of time," perhaps barely noticed when they happen, but that in retrospect can seem curiously important. She recalls missing a whole term at school because of illness; her most vivid memory of that time is reading the German fairy story "Undine," and she spends a few very interesting pages exploring why it might have so captured her imagination. She also remembers being irritated by the fact that, after her marriage to the Knight, the wild girl becomes "so gentle." In fact, the grown-up Marion concludes that the story can usefully be read as "a story about a divided or split personality."

In her next chapter, Marion explores her own experience of being in analysis, particularly her difficult, and in the end perhaps not altogether fruitful time with D.W. Winnicott. She felt at the time that "here was someone I could get into communication with, talk to, in the ways I had failed with my real father." But the situation, she soon "recognized," was unworkable: she herself was analysing a girl who was living with the Winnicott family. She cried uncontrollably when she realised that the situation was impossible, and she would have to end her analysis with Winnicott, and was angry at his reaction. Apparently totally forgetting that patients transfer childhood feelings on to their analyst, he said "he did not know I felt so strongly about him." She follows this with a Winnicott paper about "disillusion about what one gives," and remarks rather sadly that it would have saved her a great deal of time if she had been able to read it then. And she concludes this with a brief discussion of Winnicott's doodle drawings, some of which were shown in London in 1995.

One of her last chapters is called "Towards bringing bits of one's self together," and that is an accurate description of her final pages. Marion looks back and discusses some of her own doodle drawings, and writes at some length about a recent book about the Easter story. (That essay is subtitled "The need for fiction.") Still thinking about her son's picture book, she searches through Winnicott's books for a piece that she only half remembers, but knows was very important to her. It is an essay about an "intermediate area of experiencing, to which inner reality and external life both contribute. It is an area which is not challenged, because no claim is made on its behalf except that it shall exist as a resting place for the individual engaged in the perpetual human task of keeping inner and outer reality separate yet inter-related." Marion further describes it as a "space of overlap between what comes from the private inside of one's self and what is there in the shared world outside."

Bothered by Alligators perhaps falters, or rather peters out, at the end, because it remains unfinished.[4] Her mind was literally wandering, as it always did, in a creative, not an involuntary way. This state of "non-closure" was deliberate, I believe, quite consciously deliberate, for I think Marion continued writing the book to stave off death, and therefore it had to remain unfinished, until that event which is our common fate had the final word.

Nevertheless, in the context of her oeuvre, unfinished or not, *Bothered by Alligators* is a fascinating addition to her bibliography. It combines the two primary strains in her writing – the making of diaries and the analysis of images. And as the most autobiographical of her books, it might be regarded as a summation, the last words and thoughts of a writer who was continually thinking with that lively, enquiring and deliciously quirky mind, and who was also willing to take risks in her writing, by spontaneously expounding her unexpurgated thought processes.

Towards the end of *Bothered by Alligators,* she again returns to Winnicott, searching his work for a passage she half remembers, about his belief that "there is an inner reality to every individual, an inner world which can be rich or poor and can be at peace or in a state of war." Marion

Milner's search for her own inner reality, which can help us find our own, was restless. It was never quite at peace, yet neither was it at war with itself. But it was certainly endowed with riches, riches which she shared generously with us all.

Notes

1. Dr Frederick Mulder, a Canadian, came to the UK in 1968 to finish his doctoral studies at Oxford. He stayed in England to become a dealer in original prints from the fifteenth to the twentieth century and is considered a world expert on nineteenth and twentieth century European prints. He is also known as a philanthropist.
2. See M. Milner, *The Hands of the Living God*, Hove: Routledge, 2010. Introduction by Adam Phillips.
3. See M. Milner, *Eternity's Sunrise,* Hove: Routledge, 2011. Introduction by Hugh Haughton.
4. See Note on Appendix and Appendix, pp. 269–272.

A note on the text

Marion Milner was working on the manuscript of *Bothered by Alligators* right up until her death in 1998 (see Appendix and Note on Appendix, pp. 269–272).

The text here is as she left it at her death and retains such idiosyncrasies of style, spelling etc. as contained in it. Silent corrections have been made only in cases of typographical errors and occasional repetitions. Any other clarifications and minor alterations are included in square brackets (e.g. Beveridge, p. 3).

All the illustrations in Milner's original are included except for one that has gone missing – her son's passport photograph (see p. 65).

Introduction

In 1990 I decided that, now I was aged 90, it was time, belatedly, to try to get some sort of order into my papers, so as to be ready for being dead whenever that might be. In the course of doing this I found two things that I had forgotten and which gave me great pleasure. This find occurred when I had just been thinking about my son J's early years and feeling sad that owing to my husband having become a partial invalid I had had to go back to work fairly soon after J's birth, and so had not been always there for some of his earliest steps in growth.

What I had found hidden in a cluttered drawer of papers was first a little note book in which I had kept a diary of some of his conversation and main kinds of play, from the age of 2¼ to about 9. I also found a story book with pictures made by him at school, aged 7, in what looked like a weekly free period. Its title page was carefully inscribed "Published, March 1939"; that is, not many months before the outbreak of the Second World War. The setting for the diary was our house in London, which I am still living in, and which we had moved to from a flat, when he was 6 months old, in order to have a garden for him. The school was a small private day-school in Hampstead.

I got the diary typed out and showed it and the story book to a few colleagues and friends, who all said it should be published. I had agreed with the suggestion, because I had the idea that, as a book, it could show parents some of the ways in which a child can struggle with the interplay of his own and his parents' problems, and how he can do this by using his poetic intuition long before he can express the problems in direct logical speech. With this in mind, I had set out not to use any of the particular language tools used by psychoanalysts, so as to keep it readable for parents who have never read Freud. In spite of this, I kept finding that quite deep psychoanalytic ideas kept cropping up, and this made me anxious that I might really be trying to analyse my own child. However I slowly came to realise that it was not a question of me analysing him, but rather of his images analysing me. This meant that I had to go on with no idea where this undertaking was going to lead me.

On finding the diary and the story book, I had shown them to J himself, he now being a Senior Fellow at his university. He had chuckled at a few of the items but said he had no memory at all of making the story book. Later when I sent him a note telling him of the plan to publish it and the diary together with my own comments, he had phoned and said simply, "No problem."

No doubt many of my colleagues in the whole field of different psychotherapies who may read this book will see what J did and wrote in terms of their own particular models about what being human really means, including the different ways of trying to put right what may have gone wrong. However, that is not what I am mainly concerned with here, which is, or so I thought when I began the book, to try to understand more of the ways in which what William Blake called "each man's poetic genius" had found metaphorical expression for J's own joys, sorrows, angers, anxieties and hopes.

The setting

In order to understand some aspects of the diary I have thought it necessary to describe J's family situation. The first part of this account begins in 1926, when I had not yet started to write my first book, *A Life of One's Own*, and I had begun keeping the diary on which that book is based. When this diary began, I already had a degree in Psychology and Physiology, and was working in London as an industrial psychologist at the Institute of Industrial Psychology. I was becoming deeply interested in problems of concentration, and one day came across a pamphlet by a man called Elton Mayo, who was working at the Harvard Business School, about reverie in industry. I said to my boss, C. S. Myers, I would like to work with that man. He replied, "All right, I will get you a Rockefeller Fellowship for it," which he did.

I had already been granted the Fellowship when, in 1927, I met Dennis Milner. When I was on holiday in Dorset, I knew he was coming down to join me and half expected he would ask me to marry him, but had no certainty about what I would say. Then, after a small sleep following a picnic on a Dorset heath, I had woken to know that, in my sleep, I had decided I would marry him if asked. When he came the next day, we went out in his car, to draw and paint together, and landed up looking down into a quarry and at a little puffing steam engine. My drawing (which is published in my book *On Not Being Able to Paint*) was a competent realistic picture, purely representational. Which was what I then thought drawing was about. His was quite different, no shading, purely linear, and he had actually shown the puffing of the steam engine by ascending circles. That he could so easily do visual play with the so-called real world delighted me, and when a little later he said "I always wanted to go to America, let's get married and go," I said "Yes."

He was an engineer inventor, eight years older than me, and so would have been called up to fight in the First World War, but having come from a Quaker school he had taken his stand as a conscientious objector so that, when the war began (having learnt poems to support himself in prison), he was all ready to face imprisonment. However his call-up papers failed to arrive. Instead he found himself work as an engineer in a famous Quaker firm, and married a young woman, also from the Quaker school. He had become passionately interested in politics, so soon gave up his job, and, with his wife, toured the country in a caravan, standing as an Independent in the 1921 election. Though he did not get elected, he wrote a book, called *Higher Production*, explaining his ideas. Something similar to the idea he had worked out was eventually to be incorporated in the Beverage [Beveridge] Plan, many years later, in 1944.

As he did not get into Parliament he went back to work as an engineer. By now he and his wife had a daughter, but it seems that the marriage was coming unstuck, and it ended in a complicated divorce.

When we were drawing together in the Dorset quarry, I recognised that there was much in him that reminded me of my father: for instance, the shape of his head, and the fact of both being musical (my father passionately so) and both being able to enjoy being funny and being serious. My father, who had been described by an old friend of my mother's as "a very fascinating man," was a real Victorian romantic. When I was aged 11, he had a sudden and severe nervous breakdown, caused, I always used to think, by his having been sent by his clergyman father, through some family connection, to work in the Stock Exchange. Whatever the cause, the specialist had warned my mother that after it he would be very irritable for a number of years (the actual illness had only lasted a week), and this is what happened. He became irritably impatient with my mother, and this made me, in my adolescence, very angry with him, as my mother was a loving and devoted person, very modest and with a fairly literal and conventional turn of mind. I remember her once saying that she wished she was "good at something," though in fact she made, on holidays, very good water colour landscapes, what in those days was called "sketching." She was also very pretty, though she did not seem to bother much about it.

I remember struggling with my anger, not daring to confront my father with it. Instead, I pinned my hopes on the classes I was expected to attend before being confirmed into the Anglican Church, to which all my family belonged. I was promised spiritual grace from the laying-on of hands by the bishop, and more from attending my first Holy Communion service. But it did not happen; I was still angry, with a backdrop of guilt about it. So when Dennis's story of a broken marriage led me to suspect some strong emotional problems in him, this did not put me off the idea of marriage, for in a muddle-headed way, I had the thought that I could be a help to him, psychologically. Like my father, he was also quite good-looking.

Dennis and I did get married in September 1927 and at once sailed for the United States. When I first met Dennis, he had been, after his marriage breakdown, running a touring stage company for a gifted actor friend, and so he planned to write plays in America, while I did the work for which I had been given the Fellowship. Hence, during our first winter in the USA, while staying in Boston, he came across a book he thought a wonderful subject for a play. He was actually in the office of the Boston Repertory Theatre to sign the contract for him to do the dramatising when it was discovered that the copyright had not yet run out. Subsequently this book was dramatised by someone else, and became the famous film *Kind Hearts and Coronets*.

During the winter in Boston, I was attending Elton Mayo's seminars at the Harvard Business School. The other students were two research workers being prepared for what came to be called the Hawthorne Experiment in the Western Electrical Company of Chicago. In the seminars, we worked mostly on Pierre Janet, early Freud and Jean Piaget's *The Language and Thought of the Child*. I also managed to get a bit of Jungian psychoanalysis, having been given the name of a woman analyst by a Freudian friend in England, and not yet knowing about any differences between Freud and Jung. I think I went once a week for about three months, and it centred on my being an introvert, in Jung's terminology. Subsequently I heard that my analyst had gone to Vienna for a Freudian analysis.

After the winter in Boston we bought an old Chevrolet for £70 and set out across the States to go to Los Angeles where I was supposed to study the work Miriam Van Waters was doing with delinquents. The journey was splendid; sometimes we slept in the car, sometimes in what were then called motor camps, where neat little huts provided just a bed and a cooking stove.

It was in one of these, on the outskirts of Santa Fe in New Mexico, that I had an experience to do with reverie, or rather with concentration, that seemed to me afterwards to be just what I had really, unknowingly, come to America to find out about. It was, quite simply, a way of shifting one's concentrated awareness away from the struggle after logical discursive statements, which I believed was what I had been given the Fellowship for, and directing my awareness into bodily movement, in this case the movement of my hands darning socks, the result being a feeling of great joy and contentment. It seemed like a real achievement of joining up mind and body, an exciting discovery, something new happening to me. Much later, when in 1932 I set about writing up my 1926 diary, I did remember how I had, in 1926, recorded another, to me surprising, discovery, also to do with the body and a change of attention. It had come when playing table tennis, for I had found that by attending to the place where the ball should go rather than thinking what I should try to do with my arm to get it there, my arm seemed to know just what to do all by itself. But this time, in Santa Fe, it was this simple awareness of my hands, from inside, that I had found myself attending to, and not in a game, but doing something I had previously thought of as a not very interesting activity, darning socks. In fact it was to take me a very long time to make full use of this discovery, a task not even yet completed.

In Los Angeles, instead of studying delinquents we met two English painters, Jan and Cora Gordon (Jan was subsequently to become art critic to *The Observer* in London). We spent much time with them. Later Jan was to publish a book called *A Step Ladder to Painting* which he dedicated to both of us as the guinea pigs on whom he had tried out his ideas. What he said about outline in painting inspired me to make a drawing of two jugs (see my book *On Not Being Able to Paint*). The overlap of their two shapes gradually led me, over the years, to develop the symbol of two overlapping circles which was to become central to my thinking about concentration, reverie and creativity.

Often, in Los Angeles, when I was supposed to be listening to some university lectures on psychology, I actually sat in the campus under a huge gladiolus bush, watching the humming birds feeding from it, just delighting in their colours and shapes.

It was when we were half-way through our stay in the States and due to start driving eastward on the first lap of our return to England and Dennis having to decide what

Two Jugs

work he would do that he began to develop what gradually became acute asthmatic attacks.

When we did get back I returned to my previous work at the Institute of Industrial Psychology, though I cannot remember at all what I did there, while Dennis and I set about trying to find treatment for the asthma. This included hearing about the ideas of a New Zealander, Mattias Alexander, and his work on a special kind of awareness of bodily movement. We even went to see him for a consultation over the asthma, but there was too much clash of personalities between him and my husband for it to lead to anything. All this time I knew that I wanted a child, but it did not seem a very practical idea. However in 1931 I found I was pregnant and J was born in 1932.

I had not the slightest experience with babies; there had been none in my friends' families and I was the youngest in my own. Hence Dennis, rather wisely I think, found a young woman called Star, and installed her in our flat while I was in hospital for J's birth. The only baby instruction book available at the time was Trubie [Truby] King's, but we did not approve of following the book's instructions about sticking rigidly to four-hourly feeds and just letting the baby cry.

I successfully breastfed J for ten months and the weaning seemed to happen quite easily. During these months, taking advantage of the quiet time after the six o'clock morning feed, I started to write about the diary I had kept in 1926, and this was finally to be published, in 1934, as *A Life of One's Own*, under the pseudonym of "Joanna Field."[1]

Fairly soon, because of Dennis's illness, I had to go back to work, not to the Institute of Industrial Psychology but giving evening lectures on psychology to the Workers' Educational Association in the East End of London. This meant that I could be at home during the day, though I was rather preoccupied preparing the lectures, as I had never done any lecturing before.

Following this I was asked to undertake a research job for the Girls' Public Day School Trust, initially for one year, but in fact it lasted for five, until the outbreak of war meant the city schools were evacuated to the country. Because of this many of the schools were located all over England, so quite often I had to be out of London for four nights of the week, only getting home at weekends. One of the schools I visited was at Oxford.

Also during these years I wrote a book about the work (this time under my own name), called *The Human Problem in Schools*.[2] (I had used the pseudonym Joanna Field for *A Life of One's Own* because I thought some of it might upset a few of the schoolmistresses where I was about to begin work.)

It was when interviewing the girls during the course of my school research that I decided to have some Freudian psychoanalysis, fitting it in between my visits to schools out of London and hoping it might help me with the interviewing, but also, help me with myself.

Also during this time I made the discovery that by making what at first looked like a mere scribble, if I went on with it, without any preconceived idea about what it might represent, its story would emerge, sometimes completely opposite from anything my conscious mind was prepared to accept.

The fact that something meaningful could be produced simply by giving total freedom of movement to my hand and

[1] Marion Milner, *A Life of One's Own* [1934], Hove: Routledge, 2011.
[2] Marion Milner, *The Human Problem in Schools*, London: Methuen, 1938.

eye on the paper was a great surprise, so much so that I felt it called attention to something that could be being left out of the school system I had been studying. In my surprise I seem to have quite forgotten that I had not invented the method myself, but had been to an exhibition of paintings by a Dr Pailthorpe, herself a psychoanalyst, in which a great number of paintings made this way were shown. Only now did I remember coming home from the exhibition and saying to myself, "I wonder if I could do that too?" I think that these doodle drawings were shown to my analyst but I do not remember that any of them were interpreted by her.

The fact of these drawings having been made, probably in 1938–9, without any planning and yet containing so much that made sense to me, led me to try to write about them. The result was that, the very day that war was declared and I knew that my schools job was at an end because of the evacuation of the schools, I sat down under a tree to write about it. Actually what I wrote became a book, illustrated with my own doodle pictures. It was eventually published in 1950, under the title of *On Not Being Able to Paint* (still under the name of Joanna Field). A second edition under my own name appeared in 1957, with an introduction by Anna Freud and an appendix by me.

With the war getting under way it seemed likely I might be called up to do psychological work for the government, but when I told my analyst this, she suggested that I apply for training with the British Psychoanalytic Society. I was duly accepted and actually qualified in 1943, which I think was too early but officially qualified analysts were urgently needed because of so many being away doing psychiatric work for the army.

Having thus tried to give some account of the background from which the diary and story book emerged, and also see if I could understand what J might be trying to say, as I thought this might be useful to other parents, I was soon to find my aim had changed, so that the writing of this book was an attempt to see if I could use J's images to make up for what had gone wrong in my own experience of being a patient in psychoanalysis, and to see how far this could be done without the help of the analyst and the psychoanalytic couch.

PART ONE

The diary

1

The diary

When I set out to look at the diary and story book I thought I would try to study them with a quite open mind, empty of psychoanalytic technicalities, hoping that some fresh insights about what it means to be human might emerge from this encounter between him and me after this gap of more than fifty years. I therefore tried to see if I could look at the diary and the story book with the eye of common sense, as if I were a mother who had accepted the idea of there being psychic processes that are unconscious but letting my psychoanalytic ear have a rest. However, it gradually became clearer that things were happening to me as a result of this study that I had not expected.

I have reproduced the diary just as it was written in the 1930s when J was aged about 2. I had some knowledge of early Freud, particularly what he had called the Oedipus complex, but had never heard of D. W. Winnicott or Melanie Klein, and Bowlby's work on the intensity of an infant's attachment to the mother was still far in the future. What I did know about was Jean Piaget's *The Language and Thought of the Child* which we had studied in Elton Mayo's seminar at Harvard in 1928. However, the first few diary notes are in terms of body language rather than the use of words.

The black dog

(Undated, J about aged 2)
The X's came to the house with a large black dog – there had never been a dog in the house before. J started to circle

round and round it making chirruping noises, a sort of chant of delight? After this he tried to hug all dogs he saw, until warned of possible dangers.

Independence, strengthening of self-feeling

(Not dated)
Slight feeding difficulties, these suddenly improved when Star allowed him to go freely on walks, not go in the pushchair, nor with Star holding the reins. Before this change he had been recently a bit listless. Also marked need to do things for himself, for instance, he would not eat food if it had been cut up for him.

(It was in February 1934, when J was 2 years old that his father was advised, for the sake of his chest, to go to Spain for the winter. Then, in March, when my term's work was over, I went out to Spain to join him for two weeks, leaving Star in sole charge of J. We had great confidence in Star, and when we came back from Spain J seemed to be flourishing, not obviously affected by our absence. However, the next item in the diary suggested something different.)

Reaction to our absence

(J aged 2¼ after our return from Spain)
J went dead white when visiting his Grannie who lived nearby, and not finding her in her sitting room as he had expected. Left off nappies at night and often did a play of putting a dry nappy on, like a skirt.

Star's accident

(July 1934, J aged 2½)
Star, on one of her days off, had an accident. She was knocked down by a car and was unconscious in hospital for two weeks; no one knew if she would recover. We were quite unsure how to explain it to J. At first we said Star had gone

on holiday, but when J developed an artificial and flippant manner, we realised he did not believe the holiday story, so we tried to tell him the truth as far as we could. At once he returned to his usual cheerful spontaneity. Star did recover but did not come back to work with us. Instead a young woman called Bar came.

After Star left, J became frightened of flies in the garden (he had been bitten by something) but this fear disappeared when we all went to friends in the country for a few weeks. Instead, he became frightened of dogs.

Uses words for time

(1934, aged 2 years 7 months)
He uses the word "soon" and understands it; he asked for his potty upstairs, and I said "You'll have it in a few minutes." He said "soon" and seemed to be content.

Janet (a friend's child, same age) screamed at seeing a hedgehog. J said several times, "All right, Janet, all right."

After arriving from his walk he said "Want Mummy" and poked his head in. I said "J is going to have his dinner." He replied "Mummy have her dinner soon." And went downstairs. I heard him say "I was just having a talk with Mummy."

I bumped my head and said so; he began rubbing his.

Water pipes and drains, gas

Is now less interested in pouring water from one bowl to another, but still immense interest in all the water pipes in the house. Also calls the grid-covered drain beside the sandpit "J's water-hole."

Wants to know where is the smoke from the gas that heats the geyser and whether there is fire in the hot pipe.

When I lit the Perfection oil stove, he looked underneath and said, "Where's the gas?"

Helping his father

(20 August 1934, aged 2 years 7 months)
His father trying to cut something out, J trying to help but his father got it wrong and was cross. J said "Daddy cross, Daddy got it wrong."

The shut door

When I was working at my desk, he went out of the room into the bedroom where his father was ill in bed; I got up and shut the door (for warmth). He came back and said "Did you hurt yourself?" I said indignantly "No." No more answer but a few sobs.

(I now thought that the indignant insistence that it was not physical pain stemmed from his inner battle over the pain of having an ailing father and therefore a mother he was partly shut off from owing to my need to work.)

Muddle over "me" and "you"

(16 September 1934)
Still says "Me carry you," meaning "You carry me." Also "The engine pushes him" when he pushes the engine.

Lovely black or dirty black

(September 1934)
Has joy in his hands being "all black," but throws a stone away as "dirty." Also insists on being alone when sitting on his potty. Shows delight in throwing things down the gutter grid drain, into "J's water-hole."

Being helpful game

(October 1934)
J: "Which shall I get for you?"
    J: "Shall I get another kind?"
    Me: "No thank you."
    J: "Shall I get a which for you?"

He hurts a sailor

(31 August 1934, aged 2 years 7 months)
Great delight over a tin sailor he had found in someone's house, where we were visiting. He insisted on bringing it back, called it "Man." Bumped it and said "Man hurt."

"Man can't dingle" (pee)

"Man got an Albert" (penis)

"Daddy's got an Albert, a big one."

Note: Albert was the family name for penis, a joke about the Albert Memorial.

A pillow-cat

Shown a caterpillar and told the name. Repeated it as a catapillow. Two weeks later shown another and called it a "pillow-cat."

Daddy as a mender

(September 1934, aged 2 years 8 months)
J: "See'd a big clock this morning."

M: "Where?"

J: "Upstairs."

M: "I've got a little clock but it's broken."

J: "Daddy mend it – no, man mend it."

Trying to control my wants

J (cutting up an orange): "J have both."

J: "J have half."

J to me: "This is yours." (Later) "Mummy got hers." When he wanted my orange as well as his own: "Mummy doesn't want any orange." When he didn't want me to stay lying down and I insisted on doing it, he said: "Mummy wants to get up."

The animate and the inanimate

(After the zoo): "J saw monkeys all day." (Not true, only afternoon.)

(Holding toy dog): "Doggie got a tail. Doggie can't push (defecate). Doggie can't walk, no. Doggie can't bark."

Biting and tasting

(23 October 1934, aged 2¾)
While I am dressing him, says "I must not bite you, no, I'll taste you," and kissed me. Then "I mustn't cry like that" (after a little whimpering because I had gone upstairs and left him).

Alligators

I now remember something that was not in the diary, so there is no date. I overheard J talking softly to himself, saying "Poor Sara, are the alligators bothering you?" (Sara was the first name of a Mrs Taylor, who was our daily charlady in London, but who came with us to the country for holidays. J was devoted to her. She was always called Taylor in the family, never Sara.)

Being monkeys

(October 1934)
J and Janet (three months younger) sitting on the stairs. J gave a very good imitation of a monkey and insisted on his little glass monkey having some breakfast.

Star's visit

(11 November 1934)
Star was coming to visit him. Suddenly at breakfast he said, gaily, "Star is coming back, I want to talk to her, my Star." Up to this time, he had often asked for Star, said he did not want Bar. Now this had stopped. Star had been to see him just after he had hurt his foot, and it was getting better. J: "Star made my foot better. No, J did." Once when I asked him to do something he said, "I'm just thinking."

Interest in other people

(4 November 1934)
Bar told me of a talk J had with her. "Have you got a Daddy, Bar? I have got a Daddy." (later) "Has the postman had his breakfast? Has Taylor had her breakfast?"

Who has a penis?

(November 1934, aged 2 years 11 months)
(Another talk with Bar) J: "Have you got an Albert?" Bar: "No, I haven't because I'm a lady. Mummy hasn't either." J (with a twinkle): "Star has an Albert."

First telling of a dream

(25 November 1934)
J: "I went in a train last night on the railway alone."
    Me: "Anybody with you?"
    J: "Yes, a lady."
    Is playing alone with his golliwog (which he rarely takes much notice of) saying, "Darling, are you tired?" Puts two cushions as a bed, and offers to fill hot-water bottle and put it at G's feet. I went to do something else and came back to hear him saying "Duckie, J's here."

Accepting sex differences

J: (To me in bathroom) "Have you an Albert."
Me: "No." J: "Only John." (As afterthought "and Daddy.")
After defecating: "I've got a hole where I push."

Not trusting his own likings?

(January 1935, aged 3 years)
Often asks "Do I like so and so?" Me: "Yes, I think you do."
J: "Is she nice?" (As if he is unsure of the goodness of his own liking, having to have it confirmed? Even afraid of what "liking" (loving?) can do?)

Use of why?

(March 1935, aged 3 years 3 months)
He uses phrases like "I expect so," "You don't know" and "I think so" quite easily.

Fantasies

(March 1935, aged 3 years 3 months)
J: "What's that?"

Me: "A church."

J: "I climbed up a church when I was a baby and bonked the roof."

Now rides his bicycle perfectly.

Christmas and the moon, etc.

(aged 3 years 3 months)
J: "I want to see the round moon, the yellow moon."

J: "The moon is moving."

Me, as we walk: "No it's us that's moving."

J: "No, it is moving. I know. Christmas pushes it."

J: "What cut out a bit? I know. Christmas did it."

J: "The clouds turn on the rain and the sky turns it off."

Controlling the wind

(27 May 1935, aged 3 years 5 months)
J: "What's that noise?"

Me: "The wind in the trees." (A gusty day, too cold for a picnic.)

J: "I will cut off the branches, then there won't be any wind."

Being a kitten

J: "I am a pussy cat." (For the last several weeks, delighted with friends' kittens, tried to jump like them.)

Trying to keep me at home

(27 May 1935, aged 3 years 5 months)
J: "I can't let you go to Oxford" (where I am now working).
"You mustn't want to."

Bar reports he is afraid of birds, "They will come to bite him."

Broken things

(May 1935)
Again, no "why" questions.

J (looking at a broken handle): "What for did it come off?"

Me: "I pulled too hard."

J (twenty minutes later): "It's come off."

Me: "Why did it come off?"

J: "Mummy pulled it."

Another change of nanny

(May 1935)
Bar had to leave for outside reasons.

Recovery from earache

We then found another young woman, a Miss D, to take Bar's place. Unfortunately, she claimed to know a lot about "Psychology" and had too unbending principles; for instance when friends asked if J would like to join a percussion band, she said, "No, he values his freedom."

One day after about two weeks I heard J crying in the early morning (a most unusual thing) and when I went to see, found him standing between his door and Miss D's, saying that he had earache and looking as if he did not know who to turn to. I called him down, and since it was Sunday, did not have to go to work, spent the whole day sitting in an armchair beside the open window with him on my lap. He did not seem to want to talk but just sat still – and then said the earache had gone away completely. We felt that

Miss D was not really the right person, so we had to search again.

His sun-babies

(May 1935, aged 3 years 5 months)
In her place came Joyce, who was a distant relative and had a very nice sense of humour. And now there began to be notes in the diary about what J calls his "sun-babies."

For instance:

J: "I would like to have one of my sun-babies to sleep in my bed with me. They are getting quite big now."

Me: "What's its name?"

J: "I think it is J."

Later I found a note saying that Star was now working at an institution called "The Sun Babies Home."

Whooping cough

(July 1935, aged 3½)
J had caught whooping cough from a little girl of his own age who came to play with him, he had it rather badly, I noticed that after it he seemed to have changed a little, lost something.

Dying when I die

(November 1935, aged 3 years 11 months)
Saturday, November 1935. This morning his father went away to the country for the weekend. J seemed quite cheerful about it. But when I came in from a walk I found him playing with Taylor, trying to punch her and laughing immoderately. When I took him up for his rest he wanted to play "Where's J!" in the bed. When I came down, he began forced crying, and saying "I don't want you to have any lunch." I went back to him, and he roared. I gave him something to play with, but soon after he was shouting and I said he could come down. I put my arm around him and said, "You know Daddy hasn't gone for long, he will be back tomorrow. Didn't you

know?" We talked about this. Then he said, "Would you like another cushion?" and insisted on giving me two.

After tea, when cutting out pictures, he asked "What did great-Granny feel when she was getting old?"

Me: "I don't know."

J: "Did she think she was going to die? Why did she die?"

I explained that she was getting very old and probably felt quite ready. J said "I'll die when you do."

Me: "I don't expect you will die till you are quite an old man with children and grandchildren."

Being separate game

(November 1935, aged 3 years 11 months)

For the last month has been insisting on hiding behind the towels after his bath. I am to say "Where is little J?"

Me: "Where is J?"

J (hugely delighted): "Here he is!"

Then again, hiding till only his feet showed under the laundry: "Can you see my feet?" (i.e. trying it out, he can see me, I can't see him. So need not die when I do?)

His chicks

(24 December 1935)

Suddenly: "My chicks were very tired last night. They were awake when I got up this morning. Now I have put them to rest in the straw. You mustn't disturb them."

Me: "Where?"

J: "At the back of my nursery cupboard."

J (to a visitor): "Have you got a kitten?"

V: "No."

J: "Why haven't you?"

V: "Because I have no one to look after it when I am away."

J: "One of my sun-babies would do it for you, he's quite big, a man now. They live at Richmond."

Questions about his beginnings

(3 September 1935, aged 3 years 9 months)
J: "Are we in the world? What isn't in the world?"

(10 September 1935)
J: "Have you been to Portsmouth?"

Me: "Yes, when I was a little girl."

J: "Was I a baby then?"

Me: "No, you have only been alive for three and a half years"

J: "What was I when I wasn't a baby?"

Me: "You were a little seed, an egg."

J (Laughing): "Inside you?"

Me: "Yes, and you grew and grew and when you were big enough you came out."

J: "How did I come out?"

Me (gesture): "Through here."

J: "Was it very hard?"

Me: "Rather, but you managed it."

Nest building

This morning I was sitting on the floor and he burrowed between my legs as far as he could and said "This is my little nest, I'm making a nest," and then he brought cushions.

Shows immense interest in hens' eggs, wanting to see them laid, continually wanting to look in the hens' houses (we were staying near a farm on holiday).

Killing people

(5 September 1935, aged 3 years 9 months)

J: "Why does Mussolini want to kill people?"

Me: "I suppose he is a nasty man."

J: "Why is he nasty?"

Me: "Perhaps his Mummy and Daddy weren't kind to him when he was little."

J: "He ought to be like me."

Expecting me to know

(9 September 1935)
(At East Wittering) When in bed at rest time and at night has long sing-song talks with himself about all he has and new words heard. Expecting me to know, he often says to me, "Didn't you know that I wanted (so and so)?" Repeats it six or seven times to everyone he meets.

Using my hand to feed him

(17 September 1935)
Tried to make me feed him by saying he is so tired. Preferred to put the bread in my hand and lift it to his mouth than give in and feed himself.

He is not going to die

Our tortoise died recently. Asked about great-granny. Later: "I don't want to get old and get dead. Taylor, do you want to?"
    Later: "I'm not going to get dead."

We have a row

Demanded that I should hold his potty up for him to "dingle." Suddenly (I don't know why) I refused to. He screamed and peed on the floor saying I was naughty not to hold it.

    (I noted there were very few rows recorded in the diary. Probably because I did not like rows, I think there were in fact hardly any. I remember one, however, much later, during the war, when I was planting vegetables to "dig for victory" and J had started digging a big hole in the flower bed; when his father said he mustn't he went into a carpet-biting rage.)

More "before he was born" questions

(17 September 1935, aged 3 years 9 months)
Said to Joyce, "Where was I then? Was I an egg in Mummy's tummy? Is there an egg in your tummy? Why doesn't someone suck your titties? Will someone suck mine? Will

that pony grow into a horse? Will little dogs grow into big dogs? Where was I when Daddy was a baby?"

Me: "You weren't there because you grew from a seed that Daddy and I had."

J: "Oh, did I grow in the ground?"

Me: "No, inside me."

(Silence)

On the farm, seeing piglets sucking, day after day, I explained most baby creatures did, and he had too.

J: "But I had a bottle."

Me: "Not at first."

J: "Why shouldn't I have had cows' milk?" (repeated several times)

Again his sun-babies

Says he has telephoned to them at our London house, making imaginary telephone. Says he told them about his padlock. Says they were at Selsey before that, and I heard him say they are now at South Wittering.

I have to go abroad

(January 1936)

In the winter of 1936 my doctor, who was also a friend, insisted that I should take a term off from my work in the schools. I think she felt, knowing there were strains in our marriage (though not open quarrels), that what was needed was a bit of a rest from each other. Since my husband knew a family in Spain (Malaga) where I could stay as a paying guest, we both agreed with this idea. I was especially ready to accept this suggestion as I was aware of something surging for expression, a kind of continuation of what had driven me to keep the 1926 diary, but now, instead of trying to take note of the best image from the day before (which were then working days), I would now do it for all sorts of leisure activities: holidays, reading, plays I had seen, etc. So I went off to Malaga (by sea) and became deeply submerged in this task. The book I was writing was published in 1937 under the title *An Experiment in Leisure*, this also under the name Joanna Field. Perhaps it is owing to the depth of this submergence that I have no memory of letters from home, though when I was away on the schools job Dennis and I used to write to each other every day.

I could see now, though I doubt if I would have put it into words, that there were deep internal reasons for this urgent need to write once more: a deep unease, a fear even, of having got over-balanced in the direction of the discursive objective thought required by my schools job. I felt it was images I needed to get back to, though I had no idea where they would lead me, and I had not at all foreseen that I would soon be submitting myself for training as a psychoanalyst.

Looking back, I could see that this writing had in fact taken me into a very deep journey. I could now at least understand those people who are driven to leave family and friends, giving their lives to the task of wiping out their self-image. I had been led, by another kind of image, to experience the enormous expansion of perception and of spirit that could come when I managed to practise a certain inner gesture. It consisted of saying silently "I know nothing, have nothing, want nothing." But the cost was that J got no picture letters. It had not even occurred to me that I could make them, or that correspondence was possible with a 4-year-old. I had never before known a 4-year-old, except my child self who never received any picture letters.

When I got home I had no idea how to make use, in my everyday life, of the experience of having written this book (or been written by it?). In fact I hardly knew just what it was that I had been experiencing, though the book was published, as I have said, in 1938 under the title *An Experiment in Leisure*. It was in 1957 when Anton Ehrenzweig wrote a review of it called "The Creative Surrender" and later (1967) a book entitled *The Hidden Order of Art* that I began to understand a bit more what I had been struggling with, especially when he said his own book had been stimulated by reading mine. Remembering all this, there now came to mind the bit in the J diary where he delightedly tells people how he had let a wave do just what it liked with him. I wondered now, could it possibly be this special kind of surrender, combined with his willingness to make active use of already learned verbal skills, as well as his willingness to let his imagination direct his hands in active use of pencil, chalks and paint, that had led to the creation of the story book?

J's picture letter to me

It was amongst my papers that in 1990 I found part of a letter sent to me in Spain by Dennis, enclosing drawings and what J had said to him about them (see below).

First J had told his father to "Draw a volcano" and said "Send this to Mummy, for her to know." Then he drew what he called a dragon (not at all recognisable as such), adding, "Mummy will say 'what a terrible dragon!' won't she?" His father commented that "The dragon has two rows of very large teeth." J then drew more, saying, "It's a wrecked train, it's all wrecked. You'll put in that it's a wrecked train, won't you. It's for Mummy, you'll tell her won't you?"

J had added, according to the letter, "I like drawing Palawags for Mummy, for her to know, don't I!" He draws a ship with a funnel and smoke, then "I'll draw Mummy, these are her body, these are her legs. I'll draw her head (a circle). Not a very good one, I'll do another head. Her eyes, mouth" (all done upside down, now puts it right way up), adding "This is her arm – and some bread – it's a whole loaf. This is the place for the cook – they have cooks on liners! All this is for her to walk on. And this is to keep her from falling into the sea (shading round a triangle). This is a seagull, it's a funny seagull (apologetically)."

Then there is a picture of a flood. "You'll send them to her, won't you? Why doesn't Mummy send me pictures? Will you ask her to send me pictures?"

The letter adds that J had said to Joyce later: "Yes, I have sent a picture letter to Mummy. I wrote to her with Daddy." And he had put some scribbles on the sheet with the ship, saying (in an artificial voice) "These are for the babies to play with."

I now found a note by his father on the back of the picture letter recording a chat with J.

F: "Why are you so excited?"

J: "Because I just feel like it. Because I like it."

F: "Couldn't you be excited quietly?"

J: "No, I couldn't."

F: "Mummy has a birthday. Shall we draw a picture letter?"

J: "And I'll sit on your knee."

J's picture letter sent to me by his father

I felt re-reading this the awful thing was that I had not the slightest memory of sending J back a picture letter. In fact, I now suspect that my husband's letter did not arrive until I was on my way home. But whenever it was that I first read it, I certainly had no understanding of the message of anger in the letter; and the drawings were just scribbles, totally unrecognisable as being what J said they were. Also at this time, I knew nothing of the notion of an inner world in which there were the psychic representations of the outer world, one in which loved people could be blown up, devoured, drowned, etc.

Knowing nothing of all this when writing my diary after my return from Spain, it continues as if nothing special had happened.

Hide-and-seek

(29 March 1936, aged 4 years 2 months)

For a few days he has been saying he is not going to be a farmer but an engineer. Said he had sent his chickens back to Mr Brown (the local farmer). He just had two books about engineers. But now he has his chickens out again. Told his father it was "too much of a business to be an engineer." I told him it meant going to college.

Has sudden passion for playing hide-and-seek, but tries to tell me where he is going to hide. Huge delight in hiding in the nursery; and I really thought he was lost.

Picture letter to mother

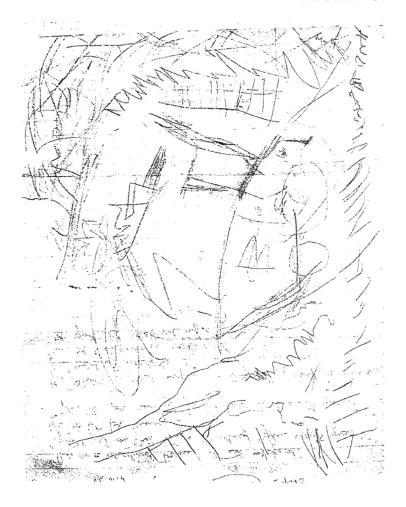

Who will hatch out of him?

(6 April 1936)

J: "Daddy, I have got a lot of chickens, I've got 100 chickens, that's more than nine, isn't it? I have got as many as Mr Leach?"

Says to me: "Go and tell Joyce I have got hundreds of chickens, that's more than nine, isn't it?" (repeats this several times)

Just before this at breakfast, had said to Joyce: "Who will hatch out of me when I am a big man?"

Joyce: "Nobody, only out of Mummies."

J: "But who will hatch out of me?"

Joyce: "The seeds."

J: "Do I put it inside Mummy? How?"

Joyce: "Ask Daddy, he knows."

J: "Do you know?"

Joyce: "Yes."

J: "How?"

Joyce: "With Albert."

J: (beams with enormous delight).

Before breakfast he drew a circle and said: "O is nothing isn't it? What words does it make?"

Sort of a boy

Recently Sylvester (aged 2½) came.

J: "He is so small. They don't know if he is a boy or a girl. He's a sort of a boy."

How was he born?

(9 April 1936)

This morning he again crawled under my knees when I was sitting on the bed, pushed his head between my legs with a beaming face saying "Where did I come out when I was a baby?"

Me: I pointed

J: "Was it warm in there? How warm?"

After pestering us with endless questions, I showed him the "Living Things" books, with a picture of a baby rabbit inside the mother. He asked how they were fed; then asked for more pictures of a man. I found one of Leonardo's on the circulation.

J: "Are little boys like that inside?"

Me: "Yes, but the drawing doesn't show Alberts and the little bags where the seeds come from. When you are big the seeds will grow."

J: "Where will I put them?"

Me: "Into a woman, your wife."

J: "How?"

Me: "With Albert, when you have got a house for your children to live in."

J: "Won't I live in this house? Where will you be?"

Me: "I'll be like Grannie and have your children to tea and you will want a house of your own."

J (laughing): "Look I've put my foot in your shoe. Will I put my foot in your shoe when I am a man?"

Me: "No, in your wife's shoe."

J: "Who will be my wife?"

Me: "Someone like Helen or Janet that you like best of everyone."

An attack on Daddy

Friday (in the bath): "Will you have another baby?"

Me: "No, I can't till Daddy is better and I can stay at home to feed it."

Going up to bed, talking about slugs, J: "What would Daddy say if I put slugs in his dingle pot?"

Me: "What would you say?"

J: "I'd laugh!" (said with glee)

Real or pretence chicks

(10 April 1936, aged 4 years 3 months)

J: "What would happen if I found a live chicken in my egg?"

Me (teasing): "It might go and join your chicks."

J: "No, my chicks are only pretence. I mean, if there were a real chick?"

I explain about broody hens, warmth needed to hatch the eggs, etc.

Very much talk about: "What would you say if ...?" "What would you say to yourself if ...?" "What would the policeman say if ...?"

His wolf

(28 April 1936)

Me: "What does your wolf eat?"

J: "Oh, flowers, lavender, sometimes grape hyacinth."

J: "Daddy, I have brought my wolf up to see you. He's been away for about a week."

D: "Where?"

J: "To see his little brother. Did I say it was his little brother? I think it was his little sister."

After lunch, when I told him he must not dig in the flower bed, because it killed the plants, he said: "But I was making a house for my wolf, he asked for it and of course he did not know, did he." Now J calls out of the window: "You mustn't dig in the beds because it kills Mummy's plants." (He has been particularly happy and serene all day.)

Later I pointed out a bee in the garden. He rushed off to make a beehive out of bits of wood. Also makes nests, says it's for his chicks to lay eggs.

Wants to draw caves, talks of his "jumping shrew" in the garden.

Now says his wolf lives in the pear tree, it is all colours, bright ones, it eats flowers.

For the last six months or so, when I put him to bed, asks: "What are we going to do tomorrow?"

Today, stamping up and down in the passage shouting: "Mummy, I've got Daddy's shoes on!"

Repeats that his chicks aren't real chicks. They are only pretence, they'll never grow up.

Reports that the jumping shrews are now all dead. Still makes nests out of sticks all over the garden.

What his wolf does

When I came home and tucked him up on Friday night he said: "Can you tell me about the bits inside tummies?" Later, in bed, after me singing him a song, he says he will sing me one: "There was a wolf and he went to Canada and shot Mussolini through the head and put him in a stew pot and ate him. My wolf often tells me things. He loves to eat animals." Just before this, he had said: "What do wolves eat? Do they eat people?"

(1 June)
Near the fairground on the Heath: "My wolf would hit the roundabout on top with a hammer." (He had been afraid of it last time.)

Where does his wolf go?

(12 June 1936, aged 4 years 5½ months)
Last Sunday on the Heath.

J: "Let's go down to the stream." (He led me round the corner to the other end of the tunnel and pulled me down the bank. "Mummy, you must come and see, this is where my wolf goes in. I want to go in the mud. I wish I had come in my gum boots, it's good to get all muddy, isn't it?"

Is now full of realistic questions, e.g.: "Why does a finger hurt?" "Would a baby find this spoon light?" "Is Wittering farther than Africa?"

At lunch today: "Could Daddy put seeds in you and you have a baby? What would happen to them after you were dead?"

Asking about a friend's baby called Angus: "What was Angus doing then?"

Friend: "He wasn't born."

J: "Oh, wasn't he hatched out of his little seed? Would Angus eat one of my chicks?"

Lying on top of Mummy

(12 June 1936, aged 4 years 6 months)
When I was bathing him: J (full of glee): what would you say if my clock said it was eight o'clock when it wasn't and I came down and laid on top of you?"

Me: "I'd say it was too early to get up."

J: "But if I lay quite quietly?"

(Of course, when keeping the diary, I knew about Freud's ideas of the Oedipal complex, but I was totally taken aback by the directness and suddenness of this manifestation of it. For "doing it quietly" obviously meant "So as not to wake up Daddy close beside me.")

Self-awareness

Much verbal description of what he is doing.

"I laughed."

"I brought bunches of flowers in, didn't I?"

"I'm dancing."

Making containers

(22 July 1936, aged 4 years 7 months)
Much making things with wood, has a small saw that he uses quite freely. Entirely alone produced a wooden bus ticket holder – two pieces of wood nailed together, and the tickets sorted out and arranged inside.

Being eaten

Fears this morning. J: "Do sharks eat people?"

"Why do they?"

"Why don't they eat little fishes, like whales do?"

Fears of little animals, even snails and earwigs. Asks, "Do they hurt you?"

Being lost

When I read him the Bible story "The Lost Sheep" he was breathless when the lamb was lost, and while listening to the next story about Jesus as a little boy, the picture of him running up the hill made him ask: "His Mummy knows he's there, does she? He'll come back?"

Unreal boasting

When seeing a man doing a hand-stand on parallel bars in the park, said "I could do that." And when I remarked that it took a lot of practice, he replied, "I could do it," and stood on a stone, saying "Look I'm doing it."

Wanting me to approve

J: "Mummy, you love me to make this box for tools, don't you?"

"You love me to plant these things, to pick those flowers and stick them in the sandpit."

Spelling versus sound of words

(23 July 1936, aged 4 years 6 months)
Gave a "letter" to Taylor with three little bits of paper with scribbles on. "That one is how it's spelt. That one is how it sounds."

More containers

Asks Taylor to bring rushes from the country as we have just read the story about Moses in the bullrushes.

Has just brought me a book he made at school, saying he has written "stories" in it. Pretends to read them. It's a farm in Canada, there's pigs and horses and fowls. "That's me and Mr Brown (the pig farmer). That's windows of the chicken houses." On another page: "That's Eli and the boy, Samuel."

Also makes other containers: a beehive, a cattle-truck, "something to hold bread for the chickens," "a cradle for the Teddy Bear," a box for his tools. He also takes his beehive into the garden, so that the bees can come and live in it. Asks me to find out how to make a loom.

My wants must be his

(25 August 1936, aged 4 years 7 months)
Still looks at me incredulously if, when he says "But I wanted it like that!" I say "But I didn't."

Dangerous lanterns

Still interested in containers, now makes "lanterns" from bits of paper on the end of a string; two were in red paper and must not be touched. "They are dangerous." (Last Christmas, wouldn't touch a Chinese lantern he had been given.)

Further play with "Hay-barns" (boxes), "chicken-houses."

Dug a hole in the lawn under the tree and burrowed like a rabbit. Only assertive play was making a sort of sling on the end of a stick to swing a stone around.

Attacks a younger friend

(After Norwich visit to friend)
Became very dependent on me, and full of questions. Hit Anthony, a younger boy, for shouting at him. On the way back in the car, said his wolf has a steamroller.

Making a stove that worked

(Seaside holiday, Wittering)
Passionately interested in churches.

Made himself a "spirit stove" out of a tin, put methylated spirits in it, and it actually worked, blue flames coming out of the holes.

Wanting to hatch a chick

Passionately wanted a "broody hen" that would hatch a little chick. Told Taylor he wanted to be a man now and put his seeds in someone.

Who will be his mate?

Very badly wants to live in the country. Keeps asking why
we need to come back. When I said we would try to get a
house in the country he said something like "when you will
be dead."

J: "I'll be able to come up to London and find a husband."

Me: "You mean a wife?"

J: "I'll marry Jonty" (a rather girlish boy aged 4½) "or
Miranda" (aged 1½), who he called that "little boy." Then
cries, "Because her navel sticks out."

A bit of nonsense

Coming back from the beach with me, said suddenly: "A
painted rabbit made of stone that you could eat. Isn't that
ridiculous," and laughed.

Calls things in the garden "snugs." Still won't touch a
snail because he doesn't like the soft part. "It's slimy."

Imperiousness

(Chat) Me: "You like Helen, don't you?"

J: "No, she won't do what I want. I want everyone to do
exactly what I want all the time."

J: "At school we are building a prison."

Me: "What for?"

J: "To put children in we don't like."

Plays with Gavin now. He's 7. "Do you know he's got a
loose tooth?" (excitedly)

Anxiety about choice

(September 1934, aged 4 years 8 months)

Very interested in clock time and at what time I or Joyce
will come. At bed-time (a near ritual): "What shall we play at
tomorrow, what do you think it would be nice to do?" Insists
on me making a suggestion when I say it depends on what
you feel like at the moment.

Being hurt

Some anxieties about the sun, after he had a bit of sunburn on his back at Wittering. Now asks why I like to sit in the sun. Chuckles happily when I say it isn't real burning, it's more like toasting.

Born without a penis?

(6 December 1936, aged 4 years 11 months)
While drying after his bath, says, full of glee, "I haven't got an Albert!"

Me: "Do you think you left it in the bath? Look and see."

J: "I think I was born without one!"

(Although I knew about the problems that all children have in coming to recognise their own gender, I saw that this must have been complicated for J, partly because of his father being unable to achieve paid work because of his asthma, so that I had to be the main breadwinner.)

The game of saying he felt he had been born without a penis had startled me at the time, but then I thought it made sense if one saw it as an attempt to provide a solution for the Oedipus conflict. Hence perhaps his glee at the idea? He need no longer be in rivalry with Daddy and the "big Albert." Also it could perhaps be an attempt to avoid anxieties about the effects of his attacks on Daddy as an imagined factor in causing his illness.

What makes him grow

Last August (1936) his father mentioned his wolf.

"He makes you grow, doesn't he?"

J: "No it's God who makes me grow."

(We were not church-goers.)

But J is very interested in churches. He didn't want to go and see Chichester Cathedral, but when we did, he wanted to go right round it. And then made Taylor take him to East Wittering church.

Trains and feeding his dolls

(December 1936, aged 4 years 11 months)
Plays mostly with trains, though he doesn't use the engine much, usually making tunnels. Today he built an elaborate one with one end closed so that it was a cave, and he was very pleased.

Also plays with dolls (Teddy and Polly), puts out dishes full of clay food, and started feeding Teddy with a spoon, saying "He's a pig, he's spitting it all out," then "It's me that's the pig really, I'm spitting it out."

Sucking

In the bath, noisily sucked his bare knee, saying "You suck milk out of people."

The other day he sucked my thumb hard and I said, "That's how you used to suck from my breast." He was delighted at this and began to suck much harder. Also began to bite, and see how hard he could bite, hugely delighted.

(22 December 1936, aged 4 years 11 months)
Said he did not want his stocking hung on the bed for fear he might see Father Christmas, so it should be hung outside.

God

(26 December 1936)
Reported talk with Taylor on bus. "The 69 bus goes to X, the 2 goes to Y, and God knows where the 48 goes. He does know, doesn't he?"

Making a timetable

Trains is easily the most absorbing game, and he wanted a timetable made. Occasionally plays with dolls; I had to write down "dolls" for the afternoon, but a few days later he said "No," though he seemed thrilled with the dolls' food I put in his Christmas stocking.

Asked for a clockwork crane from the local shops, then said I had given him the wrong one.

He is still a little afraid of dogs, but "I like some dogs."

Claiming to know my thoughts

Twice lately has said, "I know what you were going to say," or "I knew what you were going to give me."

A cruel snake

(28 December 1936)
At tea with Grannie B, he started chasing her, saying he was a snake wriggling in the grass and she hiding. Then he did it to me, saying it was a cruel snake and I must run away. After a bit I turned on him and hugged him and he said, "No, we won't play that any more."

Return of "Where's J?" game

After his bath, he likes to crouch down with the towel all over him and I have to say "I wonder what that is over there?"

Play with gun

(12 January 1937, aged 5 years)
Staying with friends, he took Christopher's gun and carried it around. Also a pistol. Frightened of the puppy and of the jackdaw that sat on people's shoulders and pecked their ears.

Attack on Daddy

(1937, aged 5 years)
At home in the bath, made a great noise. "If Daddy made a noise like that, what would you do?"

Me: "What would you do?"

J: "I'd come down and push (shit) in his face." Much laughter.

Only a dream

He tells a dream: "There was a bird-push in my room, wasn't it horrid." Then (slightly laughing) "It was only a dream!"

The man on the railway line

(12 January 1937, aged 5 in two days' time)
Much playing with trains, making lines for them and building a farm nearby. Put a little knight on the railway line, said he would not get hurt because of his armour. Another day he set the farmer on the railway line and made the train run into him. Yesterday he was making the fireman climb up the signal and sit on top, and then jump off onto the line. Said the train would not hurt him because he would lie down under it. Said this with a sly important look, not answering my questions about it.

(Since by now I knew something more about psychoanalysis, I could not help seeing in all this something of J's inevitable anxieties over his imaginings about adult sexual relationship as well as his worries about his father's intermittent illnesses. Incidentally, I remembered that his father was never ill on holidays. I even found a snapshot of J showing him (back-view) striding off manfully with a rubber ring over his shoulder, "going sailing with Daddy" and looking very much a boy.)

Wild chicks

Today he made us both tear up bits of paper to make a nest for his little clockwork bird, then built up the nest with bricks and roofed it over. He built another one with the chicks near it. He said they were wild chicks and that the bird was not really the farmer's. I said, "Aren't they too near the railway lines?" He replied, "You often have farms near railway lines."

More about his wolf

(12 January 1937)
One day I asked about his chicks and he seemed pleased to

be reminded, and said, "I still have my wolf. Did I say my chicks had gone away?"

Me: "Where is your wolf?"

J: "Oh, he's out in the garden, in the front."

Me: "What does he do?"

J: "Oh, nothing much."

Me: "What does he eat?"

J: "Oh, he really hasn't anything much."

Me: "What would he like?"

J: "Oh, dead plants and things, he hasn't any children."

Telling about erections

Told me the other day that Albert liked to be rubbed and that he did it in bed sometimes; told Joyce too, "Because he will stick up sometimes." Said to his father, "Isn't Albert rude, sometimes he will peep out of my trousers at school, he wants to see what is going on."

Perception of other people

Says "Jane is full of fun. I doubt if Ned is." (These are older children)

His wolf as peace maker

(29 January 1937)
Says his wolf had gone to Spain to stop the fighting.

What is magic

Asked for "magic" to be explained, "Rain, is that magic?" I said "No." About an hour later he said "Snow is magic" and later "Why doesn't God stop the rain?"

Being the only person

(27 February 1937)
J: "Why have we got onions again today when I don't like them?"

Me: "Because you aren't the only pebble on the beach."

J: "What does that mean?"

Me: "That you aren't the only person in the world."

J (truculently): "I think I am" (but with a twinkle).

Me: "How?"

J: "Like this," and begins to sing a song with a made-up tune about a farmer.

Flooding fantasies

(Later) "I tell myself stories, do you?"

Me: "When you are asleep, do you mean?"

J: "Yes all the time, awake and asleep."

Me: "Tell me one."

J (with much laughter): "There was a bath that fell over, the water went everywhere, right up to the ceiling."

Singing to a tiger

Often says to Taylor "I hate Joyce."

Told me he wanted to make a clay tiger (having said he didn't want to play with clay any more, "Big boys don't").

Said he had a big stick to hit Joyce with.

The squirrel and the rabbit and dancing trees

(1 February 1937, aged 5 years)

Told me a story: "There were dancing trees, a squirrel came to a rabbit in its hole, they decided to live together and had babies."

Says there is too much noise at school, as much noise "as if a house fell down on top of a drum."

Music

Says he wants when he grows up to play in a Salvation Army band. Asks for one of the Beethoven Fifth Symphony records that I had been playing, and listens quietly at the doors of the gramophone.

Farmer Brown's pigs all died

Told me, or rather sang me, a story after his bath: "There was a farmer who lost all his wheat and grounds. The rest of it is rather nasty."

Me: "Tell me."

J: "His thousands of pigs all died." (True, of swine fever.)

Some months ago he said that when we go to Winstanley, he will buy eggs from Mr Brown so that he will have money to buy more pigs, or (another time) we'd give him some eggs.

Dangerous spit

(10 March 1937, aged 5 years 1 month)

Yesterday he said he wanted to spit at Joyce to make her cold worse. At the moment, he is playing the part of good mother, looking after Teddy and Polly, putting them to bed, taking them up to rest with him.

Train interest seems to have waned the last few weeks.

Another flooding fantasy

In the bath last night said "Do you know the silliest thing I could do?" "Throw the plug so that it hit the pipe and then all the water would come rushing out, wouldn't there be a lot of water!"

This idea that the silliest thing he could do is to attack the pipes and flood the bathroom (i.e. put both of us in danger of being drowned?) reminded me of the drawing of a flood included in his father's letter when I was away in Spain the year before, so is it me that has to be drowned?

Also I now realised, with a great sense of shock, the potentially disastrous effect of my failure to talk to him about the drawings and messages in his picture letter. But I also realised that I myself had been going through a great inner battle during that time abroad.

Electrical spit

(April 1937, aged 5 years 4 months)
Home from the cottage. Spat at me and said, "That's electrical spit." Asked his father for a transformer and got it.

More about nests

(26 April 1937)
Three weeks ago saw a bee in the flowers, fetched his "beehive" in the hope, he said, of catching it. Rather worried that it did not come. Also built a "nest" saying repeatedly that he hoped a bird would come and use it. Insists that our canary might, although told often that male birds don't.

Wanted to bring home nests from the country for the canary. Wanted to take Polly (his doll) to school.

More flooding

Said with glee in bathroom: "Wouldn't it be a joke if the lavatory seat fell over and all came spilling out!"

Said he was going to put the other children on the roof and take the ladder away.

The following Sunday we start "digging for jewels," he said, to see if we could find some "old, old jewels."

Had a string with a bucket of mud on the end, hanging in his "hut" in the climbing frame, and said to me, and later to David (an older friend), "It's a mud-ray lamp."

When I ran the mower too near him, he said, "I was frightened, my bottom tickled."

Next morning he kicked me for something I had said, saying "Don't be silly." Then all quite peaceful till returned home on Friday, started frequent motions, white and rancid, till Monday.

Going to bed refused to take off his own clothes. I said, "What would you do if I didn't do it for you?" "Daddy would and I would bite your head off."

(At cottage) Pee'd on a nettle and several times asked if it would die.

(Same day) Hid my gardening tools. Shut the nursery doors. I could not get in. Later was quiet in the bath, though had been sick the night before. OK to go to school.

At Win's cottage with David, played with David alone in the barn, said to me "Go away, we don't want you" when I came to fetch them. Did the same at home when playing with a girl of his own age.

Became very cross with me, said "I could kill you if I hit you in the eye."

In the evening when tucking him up in bed, I asked "Are we friends?" J said, "Of course we are! You borned me, didn't you!"

(At the time I felt quite impressed by this, knowing that I myself tended to feel that being angry would always result in a breaking of a relationship. In fact, it was soon after this that I myself began my Freudian psychoanalysis.)

Looking back over the earlier diary entries I now found myself thinking of the number of times J had said "You do like me to do so and so, don't you?" Which seemed to indicate that he feared that if I did not like what he was doing I would go away again, even not come back. However in these recent entries he seemed to feel secure enough to say "Go away, we don't want you."

Aggression against grown-ups

(August 1937, West Wittering, aged 5½)
Open aggression against us when he has an ally, another child. Chief play with Jane (new friend) is tying up the cottage gate with ropes so that we can't get in or out. With another friend, Quentin, had a lump of mud on a string, said it was a mud-ray lamp, spat at me as a game, saying again "It's electrical spit."

Books

(Aged 5 years 8 months)
For the last six months, passionately interested in *Dr Doolittle's Post Office*. But when at Wittering his only interest was in *The Farm Shown to the Children*.

Now very keen on the Bible, but only for a little, because I could not find any more simple stories from it. Now shows great interest in *Alice in Wonderland*. I read it to him twice, and then he wanted *Alice Through the Looking-Glass* every night before going to sleep. I tried Kipling's *Jungle Book* but he was not keen, though he listened with passionate intensity to the Rikki Tikki story about the mongoose.

Omniscience

I remarked: "There are lots of things you don't know."

J (incredulously): "Are there? What are they?"

Me: "For instance, you don't know what it feels like to be grown-up."

J: "Yes I do. I know what I am going to do when I am grown-up and I know what Daddy feels like."

More babies

Tells another fantasy story, for his puppet this time, about "dancing trees, and a squirrel came to a rabbit in his hole, they decided to live together and have babies."

Asks, "Has Daddy any more seeds?"

A horrible dream

(November 1938, aged 5 years 10 months)
He asked for a party; we had ten children and he wanted them to play with their own toys, and not in games together. I got a bit impatient, he became terrified of bangs from fire-crackers. Afterwards told me he had had a horrible dream, it was too horrible, he could not tell me. I said I did not mind horrid things, he said it was a snake coming out of my eye. At the party there had been a firework snake curling up.

A hurting game

Became very violent the first week or two of the holiday, pushing and hitting and climbing on Grannie (maternal) who was staying with us. Once before I had asked "Do you want to hurt me?" He, laughing, said "Yes!" Now, when I told him not to hurt Grannie, he said, "But it's a hurting game!"

Refusal to accept his own failures

Has a tendency to say, when he does something silly – falls over or drops something – "You made me do it." No acceptance that his ideas might possibly be wrong, gives absurd explanations with a completely convinced "of course" tone of voice.

Afraid of his own power

I tried to show him how to wrestle with Jane (same age as him). She pushed him over at once and he cried, refused to use his own force.

Submission to the sea

(August 1937)
Very cautious at first when playing with his rubber ring, then found he could float with his feet off the ground. Let me pull him about in his rubber boat. Fell out into the knee-deep water and was very thrilled. He was then by himself by the shore-line and a wave knocked him over. He got up excited and delighted, telling everyone "I let the sea do what it liked with me."

Muddle over what is real and what is play

He pointed something gun-like at me and said "You are dead." I said, "All right, what shall I do?" He replied, "You aren't really dead are you? Do you feel all right?"

The Book of Genesis

(August 1937, aged 5½)
After I had read him the story of the creation from the Book of Genesis in the Bible, and explained that this was what

some people thought about God, he said, "You know, I think that's true."

Losing ideas

The other night, after again asking "What shall we do tomorrow?" and I had said, "Play bricks?" he said, "I've lost something. I had an idea of it, a little house, but I've lost it, I lost the idea of it."

The story book

(March 1939, aged 7 years 2 months)
(I now realised that this was the time when the story book was being written at school, but there is no mention of it in the diary, for we knew nothing about it.)

Being alone

He seems to have very few fears; his great passion is for going for walks by himself (we allowed this within the triangle made by the three main roads). Wanted to come home from gym alone in the bus.

Puppets play

Very interested in puppets, making them from Dutch dolls. Made his first scene, called it "A Garden of Live Flowers."

Teeth

(May 1939)
Two top front ones are out, two bottom front have grown.

Fears

Went to friends who own a farm. He was quite fearless about climbing in among screaming pigs, but cautious about touching the friends' dog who did in fact once growl and snap at him.

Theology

(May 1939)

He wanted to look at the Bible picture book this morning. Looked at one of the Annunciation, and said "Mr X (at school) says he talks to angels. He can't do that can he? Angels are in heaven, aren't they? You can't see them."

When Ethel (maternal Grannie's maid) was going to stay somewhere, she had said, "I shall be lonely without you." J said "Never mind, God will take care of you."

More dreams

Some time ago he said that he had horrid dream, that faces came at him. I said that I had those too and I just said "Boo" to them. Last week when I mentioned dreams he said "I said Boo to them and they hit me and then left me alone." A few weeks ago he told me again about a snake coming out of an eye, but this time as a joke.

Stories and films

Thoroughly enjoyed the Pooh stories. Thrilled with the film *Elephant Boy* (from Kipling's story) and said he would be an Elephant Boy when he grew up. About the elephant crying over the loss of his master, said, "They would not do that, would they?"

We were discussing why sea-horses were not able to live long in zoos. He asked why. I said "Perhaps it's like being put in prison for a lot of animals." He said, "If I was in prison and they put a lion in and didn't know it was tame it wouldn't hurt me. An animal you've tamed likes you better than anyone else."

People

(22 May 1939, aged 7 years 4 months)

Joyce reports he said, "There is more than one person in the world, isn't there?"

His father's bad weekend

(May 1939, aged 7 years 4 months)
(It was here that his father, now himself in psychoanalysis, had his most severe asthma attack, having morphine injections, with his doctor visiting him thirteen times during the weekend. J would have been downstairs with Joyce or out in the garden, so probably did not see his father struggling for breath. However, the diary records J's reaction to this weekend of extreme family tension.)

Reaction to his father's bad attack

(22 May 1939)
J asked Joyce to smack him. He said he was sure he had been naughty. Smacked himself, saying "Ow!"

Who is naughty?

Very indignant on Sunday morning because he said Joyce had threatened to smack him. I said, using his word, "Perhaps it was naughty of her but we are all naughty sometimes." He said he never was. I said I was, but he would not believe it.

To kill a baby sister?

Came back from school today very truculent, threatening Taylor. Said that If he had a baby sister he'd bully her to death because Jeremy's sister had taken the house he was building.

This morning when grumbling why he could not see Daddy more, I said I could not do much with Daddy either. He asked quickly, "What do you mean?" I said, "Go out with him." J said, "But you and I can do things together, can't we?"

LONG GAP IN THE DIARY, AFTER HIS FATHER'S BAD ATTACK, FROM MAY TO 14 JULY.

Terror of a doctor

(July 1939)

Owing to J's marked change in mood and behaviour after his father's bout of acute illness we decided to get some treatment for him from a Child Guidance Clinic. There is nothing in the diary about how long this went on, but there is a note from the psychoanalyst who was working with him, which says, "He showed unusually extreme anxiety at first, quite explosive, but much less later, with developing material, not stagnant or chaotic, with definitely recognisable themes." Of course at the time we had not yet seen the picture book with the retaliating farmer killing the fox who killed the farmer's cock. I think the school must have kept the book and only returned it when, with war imminent, it was clear that the school would have to close, and there were no plans for being evacuated. I have no memory of the book being brought from the school, or of reading it. Perhaps with so many anxieties about the looming war, it remained unnoticed, only to turn up much later in the course of sorting out my old papers.

(July 1939)

Not only did we not know about the story of the dangerous farmer and the fox, we also knew nothing about the devoted porter setting himself the task of cleaning the engines, a story written only about two months before his father's acute attack. Hence the porter's imagined reparative efforts must have seemed a futile attempt to make amends for the triumphant notion of dirtying his father's face, which had been recorded in one of the early years of the diary. Thus when he hit himself and said "Ow!" it looks as if he could be trying to say he feels the illness is partly his fault, and he must therefore punish himself.

The diary continues, but the fantasies recorded in it must have been to some extent influenced by his experience during the very short time he had at the clinic. Short, because we were so soon having to leave London, because of the war.

A deliberate lie

(14 July 19389, aged 7 years 6 months)
J said, "X wanted to play with my electric motor, I told him
it was broken. It would have been if he had played with it."
Here I remembered how Piaget had once said it was a great
step in mental development when a child tells a deliberate
lie because it indicates that he has recognised the nature of
a thought, i.e. that it can be mistaken.

Need to be controlled

(July 1939)
On some train journey J pestered me with questions.

Me: "I really can't answer any more questions!"

J: "You'd better say 'Shut up' but you mustn't say it
crossly."

Need to oppose

(July 1939)
Father: "J, go downstairs." (said crossly)

J: "If you say 'Don't go downstairs' then I'll go." And he
went.

Anger and tears

J: "Do you know, when I am angry I cry, and that worries
me."

Lamps

Since last summer makes candles and lamp with clay. Went
to the British Museum to see Roman lamps.

Phantasies of power

(Wittering, August 1939)
Overheard talking to his friend Ronald, aged 7. "Wouldn't
it be nice to be full of push" (faeces) "till you swelled and

swelled, got enormous, if you bumped into people you'd knock them over." Then he said he could eat Ronald but Ronald said there would be no room. A week later, said the same thing to me when I had been reading him the Grimm fairy-tale about the six servants, one of whom drank up the Red Sea. J laughed tremendously and talked about being so fat. I said, "As fat as someone who is going to have a baby?" and then he said that he would eat me up too, and all the people at school, Miss M even, "because she is an ass – but not my friends." I said, "What would I do inside you?" J said, "You would have the other people to talk to." Me: "What others?" J: "Oh a hedgehog and …"

Wittering

(12 September 1939)
Not at all keen on going to the beach, but quite happy when he gets there. Sings to himself when floating on his rubber ring, willing to go out of his depth, but very hard to get him to go into the water at first. Digs happily on the beach at East Head where there are no waves, but guess that it was the waves at high tide that put him off. But still passionate about Mr Brown's farm, watching the threshing machine. Collects corn heads and threshes them himself very busily.

Loves cooking, made several blackberry puddings for us, insists on helping us all. Asks who put the ring on the ring plover's neck? I said, "It grew, or the ring plover did it." J: "No, God did."

Now remembered that his father, quite asthma-free as always on holidays, spent much time in a sailing dinghy we had rented, exploring Chichester Harbour, though he also came on family excursions in the car, such as to see Chichester Cathedral.

Cleaning lamps

(12 September 1939)
Wanted to clean all the lamps in the cottage, insisted on buying a new one. He wanted one at night in his room, made a very successful lantern, gave it away when we left.

Shouting out at night in his sleep and crying. This stopped a few days after getting back to the cottage.

Being a monster

(September 1939)
He and I went for a picnic; he wanted to talk about the consultation at the clinic. He said the doctor had said things that weren't true, i.e. that he thought his "Albert" might shrink. He denied being bothered about his Albert in any way. Went on burning dry grass with a cigarette, then said he was a monster that ate people. Finally, that he only ate robbers, and carried good people on his back. (I noted that there was no mention of their having talked about his anxieties over his father's illness.)

Reading and laughter

Had both the Lewis Carroll books for the third and fourth times, also both his Pooh books. I tried him with Kipling's "Elephant['s] Child" (from the "Just So" stories) and he went into fits of laughter over the last bit where the Elephant's child gets his own back on the adults; though he did not want the story again when I suggested it.

When Taylor fell into a ditch he said, "I'm sorry I laughed but it was so funny."

He asked, "Do policemen ever do naughty things?"

Playing with fire

(September 1939)
Making huts in the garden with David (an older boy). Great delight over play with candles and matches.

When his father said something in the fire looked like a monster, J said "I used to think things could be monsters." I tried reading him "Aladdin's Lamp" because it was all about lamps. He said it was a most marvellous story, but when I asked if he wanted to go on, he pretended not to be interested.

The Jungle Books

More of Kipling Jungle Books. Adored the Rikki Tikki story, read twice, then asked for Mowgli and his Brothers, seemed to love the bit in the cave when Mowgli arrives. Got stuck after the killing of Shere Khan, the tiger.

Move to the country

(October 1939, Elsted)

Now owing to the war having started, although as yet no air attacks on England, the whole family (including Taylor, but not Joyce, who was to be called up) moved to a borrowed cottage in the country. Since we now had to carry gas-masks, London had not seemed to be the best place for anyone as seriously ill with asthma as my husband was. J seemed happy in a little private school close by. His father was free of asthma, and was designing a new kind of boat. Taylor was happy with us, and I was delighted to be living in the country after twenty years away from it, and with time to spare, at least for a little while, since my schools job had folded with the war. Instead, I bicycled about the countryside, with hedges full of hips and haws and even pink spindle berries, looking for a cottage that we could buy.

Anxieties about growth and babies

(2 November 1939)

Asked for the Kipling Elephant Child again, then read it to himself. Asks, "Can people have babies when they want to?" Had been telling me, with many giggles, about a girl at school whose gas-mask was too big, although it was the smallest size. Asks "Is my head very big?" And then about a girl who said she was 15 and had stopped growing, but then grew again. "Do people do that? Do you know any dwarfs, dwarf men? Why don't they grow?" Then asked about his father's first wife's baby being born dead. "But Daddy then had a good one, didn't he? Was it his fault or hers? What happens to babies with no mother and father?" (He knew his playmate girlfriend at Wittering had been adopted.)

A bun that eats the eater

J told a story he had made up at school: "A boy ate a bun and then the bun began to eat him, inside, then he was sick of it and went to bed."

Grimm's fairy-tales and Woodcraft books

(28 December 1939, Elstead)
Still breathless over Grimm's fairy-tales, particularly the man with the nose that grew and grew. He did not like "The Juniper Tree," read it to himself and did not finish it, or "Elfin Grove," said it was so sad. He devours the Woodcraft books by Seton Thompson.

Comics

Told me a story from one, well and dramatically; about a baby elephant who stole jam, then hid from his mother in the copper and came out all shrunk.

A machine can't pray?

Tells a story of a little boy supposed to be saying his prayers who said he had "conked out." Adds, "An electrical machine can't say its prayers can it?"

Christmas

For the first time we went to church on Christmas Day. J not very keen to go, seemed anxious about it. No comment afterwards except "Canon S did the service all right, didn't he?" Had trouble thinking about presents to give, needed my suggestions. Terribly excited about tying them up. On his own idea, dressed up as Father Christmas and gave out little parcels to the evacuee children.

Becoming more aggressive

Said to a friend, Alfy, after a snowball hit him, "I'm not very good at fighting." But is very much more aggressive at home, truculent and cheeky. Laughs delightedly at the slapstick aggression in the Grimm story "The Two Brothers."

Magic rabbit bone

After reading the "Two Brothers" tonight we had a bit of a row because he was so all over the place. I came up to help him to bed (he usually puts himself to bed now). He had a rabbit leg-bone that he sawed in half; pointing it at me, he said, "I am safe from being told to be quick," then touched me with the other half and said, "You are dead." Me: "Forever?" J: "No this half (touching me again) brings you alive again." After washing he put both bits side by side to show me and said, "Guess which is the bad half." I guessed right, the misshapen half was the "bad" one.

Possessions

(8 January 1940)
His father and I gave him a little sermon about not swanking about his possessions to the evacuee children. He had just told them he had eighty-six books(!?) I seem to have said, "You don't like people because of what they have, do you?" J: "Yes." Me: "David, for instance?"

J: "Yes I do, he has got a steam engine!"

Careers

Says he wants to be a builder, not an architect.

Manners etc.

Very truculent, orders people about in an imperious tone. Was able to modify it when I said, "That's very rude." After that, he said to me, "Leave those comics where they are."

One day he threw a towel over his head. I said, "You like to be a pest don't you, a mosquito!" J: "No, I don't, I like to be nice, but it's so lovely throwing things over."

Also in the mornings he says he's stuck in bed, can't get up, but wants me to come and pull him out.

Joyful destruction

He used to cry when he broke things but the other day he threw a great slab of ice and revelled in the smash. Tonight saw a hole in his pillow. I said, "Don't tear it further," J: "I'd love to."

Anger with father

Says "Daddy always want to make me angry." This refers to his father playing billiards with Alfy when J wanted to play something else with him.

Losing his temper in games

Tried Halma, wanted to knock over the board when his father and I played. I promised a prize ("The Lively Youngsters" book) if he could play three games without losing his temper. He tried first playing against himself, but could not maintain it, insisted that one side was me, and made me lose. This was six weeks ago, now no more talk of Halma, but has bought the book with his Christmas money.

Chores

It seems he feels our demands that he should do his fair share of chores etc. are an attack from fierce unjust parents, that must be resisted at all costs, though he loves to help over non-routine things like going for the post, or lighting visitors to their car.

Opposites

Likes to play at me saying the opposite of what I want him to do, and then he will do it. Sometimes has a mischievous "I-don't-want-to-be-good" look.

Rudeness

(January 1940)

He has given up lighting the fires, won't fetch wood by himself, answers back, cheeks us, likes to torment the cat, lolls about in bed instead of washing. Tonight I lost my patience, told him I had decided not to help him wash as it makes him play the fool and gets me cross. He agreed, rather remotely, said I was interrupting his reading. I said "That's rather rude," and "Do you want me to stay up till eight or to read to yourself?" J (most quickly and politely): "I want to read to myself, if you don't mind."

This morning he said, "You've got to show me my report, mind you." I said, "I don't do anything for anybody who says "mind you."

More magic

(January 1940)

He touched me with a stick and said I was turned into a fish, and then I would be caught and eaten.

He grumbled about the frost. I said, "I can't arrange it, you must ask the Clerk of the Weather."

J: "Who is he? Doesn't God arrange it? Or is it just the wind? I'll go and ask Mr West Wind."

Keeping Taylor inside

(8 January 1940)

Wishes he never had to "push" (defecate). Wishes he had not got "a push place."

Asks Taylor what would happen if he hadn't got one?

Taylor: "You'd get rather nasty inside, you wouldn't live long, there would be an awful smell."

J: "I would not mind that – I'd like to have you inside me, I'd talk to you, but you would not have to talk to me."

Taylor: "When there were other people there, wouldn't you?"

J: "If I went to Africa with you inside me, what would you say?"

Taylor: "If I were inside it would not make much difference."

J: "I'll make some little cellophane windows for you. I think of this almost every night."

I thought then that the nightly preoccupation of taking Taylor with him, inside, must have had the advantage of her being the one person always there, neither going off to work like me nor getting ill and going to bed like his father. Apparently he had added, "But you would have someone to talk to." "Who?" asked Taylor. "Oh … a hedgehog," J replied. I thought what an apt symbol for psychic pain, a hedgehog inside, giving a pang whichever way you turn.

Foreseeing that his tastes will change

(12 February 1940)
Loves the jokes cut out of comics, sent by a friend. Wants to stick them in a scrap-book – even the ones he doesn't like now, "because I may come to like them later on."

Denies there are any unknowns

Discussing the body, I said there was much we did not know about how it works. He refused to believe this: "We do know about it." He asks what "fainting" means. Says he does know what "unconscious" means. Asks what "tact" means.

Laughter

(February 1940)
The things he laughs at in Grimm are the aggressive acts: the cudgel in the bag story, the bear in "The Two Brothers" who knocks down the guards in the palace.

Jealousy of fathers

(12 February 1940)
Took Samson (the cat) round to see X's kittens. They spat at each other. J said it was because Samson was like the kitten's father and "cats are jealous of their fathers, aren't

they!" Again, this afternoon, said the little one did not like Samson because he was bigger.

"Samson has been going courting lately, he is just old enough." Said to Taylor when he was going upstairs to see me, "I'm going courting."

Coping with a bad mood

Cried because I had turned him out – said "I'll go and see Alfy and see if he'll amuse me."

Me: "Perhaps he is in a bad mood too?"

J: "Then I'll amuse him as well."

Today he actually offered to help make Daddy's bed. He asked about the cloven foot at the beginning of the Bearskin story. (In fact the devil is the helping figure in the story.) His father began saying that he keeps his devil on a chain but lets him off sometimes. I said, "We all have a devil of our own." J replied, "Yes, I know about that." (His or mine?)

Grimm again

Loves "Thumbkin," wants it over and over, guffawed over the giant's attack on people. Loves "Golden Beard," about the boy who is Love's child and gets the princess, in spite of the jealous father.

Anxiety over compliance

(May 1940)

Moved to Harting (next village) to a cottage of our own. Fierce refusals at any suggestions of nail-cutting, hair cut or hair brushing. Insists on wearing thick blue sweater (David's) and thick blue stockings although the weather is very hot. Returned to the fear of flies that he had after Star's accident. I note that he seems to feel that to help his parents, do what we want – chores, housework, etc. – feels like utter annihilation? Is his self-surrender impulse something too strong to be accepted, for instance his joy in giving in to the wave, letting it do what it liked with him?

Hard to accept his limitations

Now very interested in throwing stones, but says he wasn't aiming when he missed. Told Granny that he knows more about electricity than his father.

Another row

He moaned and fussed about not being allowed supper downstairs. Why? I got angry and said I wouldn't have it. He said I was muck. I threatened "no supper." He cried and said he was sorry. Then got angry again, said "I tell people I like my father best." I said, "That's all right, for a boy." Then he got quite happy while I read to him "The House of Arden," and said, "Good night, Mummy dear."

Next day at lunch, suddenly said "We did get cross yesterday, didn't we, but it's all over, forgiven and forgotten isn't it! It's good to get cross with each other sometimes, isn't it?"

***

(June 1940)
Now there is a big gap in the diary. Because of the bombing fears, Mrs S., the mother of some friends of J's at the little school, said that, as she had been offered a house in the United States for the duration of the war, she was planning to go with her daughters – and would we like J to go with them? As the Battle of Britain was in full swing, and we were fairly near the South coast, we did not feel we could say "no," so we all set off for the nearest city (Portsmouth) to get J's passport photo.[1] To me it seems to show a manfully struggling look of "If I must go, I must go."

Mercifully the photo was never needed, because, after months of delay getting the necessary papers, Mrs S. suddenly rang to say they had decided not to go, and we said we had made the same decision for J. Soon I had to be in London during the week; our house there had survived the bombing with only minor damage.

[1] This photograph is missing.

Play aggression

(The next diary entry was not until two years later, May 1941, J aged 9 years 4 months , and headed "Play.")

He was very slow getting ready for bed. I said, "I'll come and cuff you if you don't hurry up." He was delighted. When I came up I pretended to do so. When he was in bed and I went to kiss him, he would not let me but hid his head under the blanket. I pretended to cry, he was again delighted and said "Serves you right!"

(Here I well understood why I had made a note of this; it was a kind of play aggression that I could never imagine having happened between myself and my own parents. It also occurred to me that my ability to do it now could be a by-product of the intermittent psychoanalysis that I had been experiencing during these last few years.)

Invention

(June 1941)

J: "I wonder who invented bacon."

Me: "I don't know, I suppose someone had the idea of salting pork."

J: "I expect God put the idea into his head."

(July 1941)

Said last night that he can see pictures in his head, not with his eyes, could see all the rooms at school. (Where he wrote the story book.)

I now found a few more notes in the diary: for instance there was one for August 1941, on holiday in Wales (he was 9).

J: "But surely I can be rude to my mother." I said, "I'll go out until you feel better." He recovered spontaneously.

A note in September reads that during some discussion of the Anglican Church's Prayer Book, J had asked what the General Confession is. Apparently I said, "Some people want to say they are sorry for things they have done that they feel they should not have done."

J said: "I'm not sorry for things."

School clothes

(Still August 1941, aged 9 years 7 months)
Now the notes relate to the next problem, which was
boarding school. The nearest available was the preparatory
part of a grammar school that was just too far to be reached
by bicycle from our cottage.

Sulking

Having been to the nearest town to buy his grey school
clothes, we found, driving back, a pine branch blocking the
road. While we tried to pull it away, he tried, more and more,
to control everything, being extremely bossy. I found myself
too much wanting him to be the kind of boy I wished he
would be, but he went into the car and sulked. Soon came
out when his father had the bright idea of using the jack
from the car to move the branch.

Visiting J at school

The next entry (15 October) is about the only visit we were
allowed to make to see J at school. Taylor came with us.)
     J (after a big hug): "It's awfully nice to see you."
     Then over a picnic tea on the Downs, when I asked if
he wanted anything more to eat, he said "I have lost my
sense of whether I want any more or not. I always used to
know." Then came a long tirade about the headmaster of
the grammar school, Mr L. "He's a liar, he's mad. Always
making new rules. Not seen him at all, except the first day.
I asked him what are the rules and he said there are few
and they are kept, but just the opposite is true, there are a
great many and they are not kept. But there is something
to be said for being with other boys. The lady who teaches
painting is sensible, anyway, gave us large sheets and said,
'Now you can make a mess.' Even boys who have been there
a long time hate it, even some of the prefects say 'He is a
brute, I'd like to spit at him.' One of us said 'Try throwing a
stone, now, and perhaps you will feel better.'"
     After telling how Mr L was a liar, J added "He said you
could come twice in a half-term to see me, whereas it's only

once a term." He added, "The lessons are rotten, it's a mad way of teaching arithmetic. The food is good but it's the only thing L doesn't do. It's marvellous to have an apple."

I was aware here that I had never known J so verbally angry as he was with Mr L, including the wish to spit at him (even though he had once spat at me and said it was "electrical spit" that could kill me). But now it was Mr L who was the cause of the too-long separation from us, only one visit in the term. So I realised more and more, with horrified shock, how totally blind I had been to the intensity of his anger over separation, something that I had then never read anything about.

1942

Next, in the spring term, J caught flu, which developed into pneumonia, but we were able to nurse him. He was never seriously ill again.

After this, we found he could bicycle to a small station and get a train to school, so he went back as a day boy – until we heard of a small prep school run by an enlightened headmaster, but now evacuated to the West country for the duration of the war. There he seemed to be happy, and there are no more dated diary records, only one vivid memory of meeting him at Paddington station for the holidays, and finding he was carrying a little cage with a white mouse in it, which he said he had taken from another boy who was ill-treating it. He also told how they had done some acting at school, in Shakespeare's *As You Like It*, and he had been given the part of melancholy Jacques. He said he was not at all good at acting, and that "God did not intend him to be more than one person."

Not sad enough

Soon among my papers I discovered a letter from him telling more about this.

"I was rather annoyed yesterday. Mrs S (mother of one of the boys) came and watched and afterwards said I was not sad enough, and that I did not know what I was talking about. I felt like saying to B (her son) 'You tell your mother to mind her own business and I will mind mine, even if she is an actor.'"

This must have been shortly after I had told J about the breakdown of our marriage, so it is likely that he was feeling too sad to know how to act sadness. In fact, when I had told him, he had cried a bit but had not said much, nor had I, I think I was not yet ready to discuss the reasons with him. Geographically the break-up was fairly simple; it meant that Dennis lived in the country with Taylor to look after him, while I stayed in London. J could be with either of us, as and when he wished. The decision had been mine. Dennis and I had had many enriching times during our sixteen years together, but I had come to the conclusion that it could not go on, and that we had both married for the wrong reasons. Dennis married again, for the third time, a few years later.

Notes on books read

He now enjoys *Treasure Island*, but it could not last the winter. The same with *The Invisible Man*. Has added *The Old Curiosity Shop*.

Questions

Questions at Christmas after his first term at the prep school evacuated to the West country. "What happens when you go to sleep? Is it just that your eyes close?" In bed, after reading about how savages make fire: "How does rubbing friction produce heat?" While hoeing the rose bed: "How does the energy get to your muscles when you move?"

PART TWO

The story book
and plate section

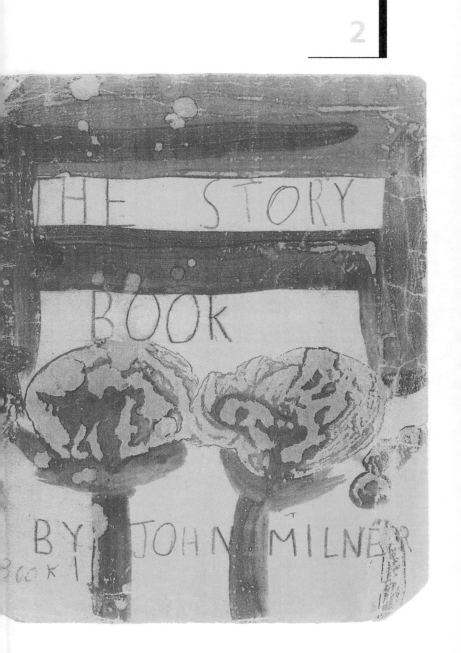

THE STORY

BOOK

BY JOHN MILNER

BOOK 1

PUBLISHED MARCH 1939

1

4

6

$\pm$8

10

11

12

13

$1\frac{1}{3}$
$\frac{24}{28}$
$\frac{23}{30}$

The farmer

Once upon a time
there was a farmer
with only two
chickens and only
one pig and only
one cock.
one day the cock was
killed by a fox The fox
was
killed by the

2 farmer. Then the
farmer thought
he would set five
traps. for the foxes.
Eight of the foxes
were killed and
eight rabbits were
killed in three.
And ves snares +

4? The woman

Once they¹ was a
woman who lived
in a house the The
woman was a
very cross grumpy
old woman She
threw stones at
lots of people

5

6† The Kittens

Once upon a time there was a kitten. The kittens mother was dead The kittens lived at home His house was a very comfortable house

7

great the boy

Once upon a time
there was a little
boy who lived
in a wood and
he lived in a
little house and
the house was
very comfortoble

10 + the boat

Once the rewas a boat. There was a man on the boat. The boat rocked and rocked and rocked. Then the man nearly fell off. He climbed on to the side of the boat

11 † The fox

once there was
a fox The fox lived
in a little house
Then the fox
decided that he
would change
his house The new
house was a
very comfortable
house the old

12 #

house was very
un comfortable
The END house
onto they and the fox
a boy and was,
a boy who lived
in a hollow tree
The hollow tree
was nice and
comfortable and warm

13 + The train

Once there was
a train and it
was always going
puff puff puff
There was a man
sitting on the
safety value When
the safety value
went off the
man was blown off

14

L M S

15

Once the four boats there was a boat with three people on it and one child and the childs name was Twink Twink liked playing with the dog who was called Bobby

16 Tink!

wet
sand

Bobby Fink tried
to jump onto a
passing life boat.

said

.2

wet

wet

sand

18 The light house
keeper was
putting five new
wicks in the oil
lamps and ten
new candles in
the lanterns.

19

The lighthouse
keeper had
finished putting
all the new
wicks and
candles in the
lanterns

20

He was putting up
the lanterns on the
wire rope in between
the two lighthouses
Bobby Tink and
Twink were playing
on the lighthouse
stairs The lamps
were lit because the
Stairs were always
dark

21

Bobby Tink was
having a lovely
time on the stairs
and one of the
oil lamps was
blown out and
Twink came out
and lit it again

22

Three people and Twink were playing dominoes on a table on a ship. The light house keeper asked if he could join in the game. Twink said he could. The people

thought it was
great fun

The + Caravan

Once there was
a caravan It
moved once a
year and only
went five miles
at a time
the boy in the
caravan thought

that it was great
fun to make a
hut in the ditch

126

The caravan
was in a field
The field was

3rd March 2nd
acres

27

28 +

Once there was
a train It went
104 miles each day
The train was a goods train
The goods were
mostly coal and
oil

Once there was
a bus the bus
went over
westminster
Bridge 3 times
a day The bus
went over Battersea
Bridge 4 times
a day

Mar
9th

1 Once there was
2 a porter and
3 he lived at the

4 station hotel
5 The porter had to
6 get up at 5 o' clock
7 in the morning

32

8 The porter was
9 putting water in
10 all the engines
11 He was cleaning
12 out the boilers of
13 all the engines
14 he had been
15 putting water in

The porter's job
was to turn on
the gas lamps
at 5 o'clock and
another job was
to make up the
waiting room
fire. He often
used to sit in

34

the cloak room
when he had
no other jobs to
do. when The
train came in
to The station the
porter had to help
the passengers off
because the step was
rather high

One day an ex-
press came into
the station and
the parter did
not have to
help the passen
gers off this time
because the train
step was a lower
step

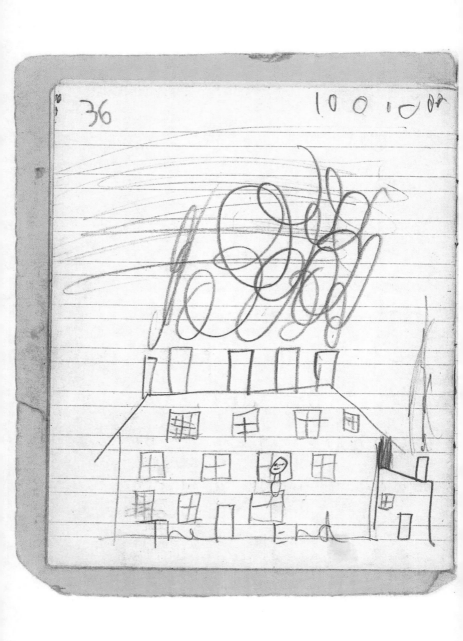

The End

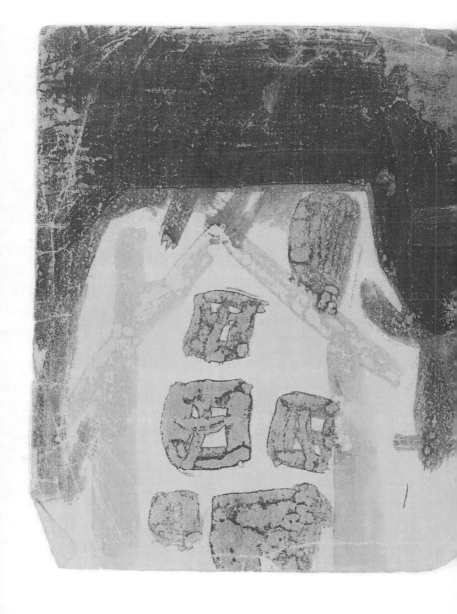

Plate section

The plates here are discussed in Part Five, 'Making collages', pp. 189–198.

The temperamental hen (see p. 189)
The listeners (see p. 190)
The Green Baby (see p. 194)
Woebegone (see p. 196)

The temperamental hen

The listeners

The Green Baby

Woebegone

PART THREE

Thinking about the story book

My first thoughts about the story book

The farmer and the fox

I now set out to try to summarise for myself the stories with their pictures, partly to see how far these might relate to the diary, but mainly I was concerned to discover what it might be that J was trying to tell the world – or himself – in writing the stories.

Thus the first story, just called "The Farmer," tells of how the fox killed the cock and the farmer then killed the fox, and also set traps by which he killed more foxes, as well as killing rabbits with snares.

On the opposite page (page 3) is the house with four chimneys belching black smoke, and most of the house is also black, the other part being rosy red. Below, in foxy-coloured chalk, is the fox with a very long tail, not at all dead.

Ostensibly the written story is about killing for food; the farmer needs his chickens for his livelihood, and the fox is hungry, perhaps starving. However, in the picture the fox is not dead, and shown behind him is a chicken with three chicks.

Although, as I have said, I had set out on the study hoping to use as little as possible the psychoanalytic language in which I had been trained, I could not help seeing this story in terms of the Oedipus myth that Freud had used when trying to find ways of talking about his own discoveries.

Thus, if you assume, as most observers of children's drawings do, that J's houses represent his self, then all that black smoke from the chimneys must surely depict a fiery anger inside his house self. Seen in these terms, this first story can be looked on as illustrating Freud's observations of what he named the Oedipus complex, the idea that the boy child secretly wishes to kill his father (or his potency) in order to take sexual possession of his mother. Seen in these terms, the farmer-father's cock is destroyed so that the son-fox can have chick babies with the chicken-mother. Giving strength to this idea is the fact that, in the picture, the chicken-mother and her babies are shown within a faintly drawn shape that could be a protective cage, while the black smoke does indeed suggest that J's fox-self has been furiously angry with the farmer-father for his possession of the chicken-mother. However, I did wonder about the fact of only three-quarters of the house being black and the other quarter a loving rosy red. Does this perhaps indicate a doubleness of feelings about his father? On the one hand, an appreciation of him, for his father really was good to him, taking trouble to teach him use of tools in carpentry, and being a comfort to him when I was away – as for instance after the picture letter to me in Spain, J says he will get on his father's lap.

Undoubtedly, therefore, the stories begin with ideas of life and death, and also of sources of sustenance. The farmer is good, providing food for his household and perhaps others, but he is rather poor and has very few animals, so the wild things that threaten his livelihood have to be trapped or killed. However, this is not the whole story, for in the picture the fox is certainly alive.

The stone-throwing woman and the see-through house

Next is the story called "The Woman" (page 4) which says she lived in a house with only three unequal-sized chimneys, no smoke, but two staircases which can be seen from the outside, so it is apparently a see-through house. There is one small head showing at a ground-floor window on the right side of the house.

Under the story of the stone-thrower is the little drawing of two shapes, one is heart-shaped but it looks a bit hurt by the impact of the other shape (a stone?) hitting it. Hurt but not broken?

There are also cat-like shapes shown at one of the windows of the see-through house, and a number of obscure coloured forms, together with, on the ground floor, a little man who has one eye blacked out and a rather grim-looking mouth. Here I had to ask myself, who is this cross stone-throwing woman? Of course it could be that it was felt to be me, the result of denying some of his own angry moments, put into me because he was afraid to know them as his own anger. But what if it was not only that, what if it really was also a bit of me that he was aware of and that I was not?

At first I jibbed at the idea of myself always throwing stones at people. But on further thought I remembered that when the stories were written, I was at the beginning of intermittent psychoanalysis, and so really having to face the fact that there could be such a secret part of myself, one that I was totally unaware of, since it did not fit in at all with my idea of myself. In fact, I was very rarely openly cross; it was one of my main problems, having great difficulty in expressing my anger.

But if this were indeed true, if the cross stone-thrower is also me, there was certainly much more to be said about it. I therefore decided to go back to the kind of writing I had found useful in my first book, not struggling for logically correct order but letting come what may.

"Those two shapes at the bottom of the stone-thrower story, they do look like stones and one is like a heart, though a slightly misshapen one. To throw away one's heart because it can hurt too much trying to avoid its pain? Afraid of it getting broken? But in the story, it's the other people who are hit by the stones, who get the pain. And why does she do it? Perhaps even to pay them back? But I didn't invent her, she is J's creation, a sort of inner pantomime figure. And if it is partly his own wish to throw stones at me, it must be because of feeling how heartless I did sometimes seem to him? But as I remember it, he was never a difficult child. His attacks (says the diary) often appear as questions ("What if I did so and so?") expressed as possibilities, i.e. he could kill me "if he hit me in the eye." But open anger, no. Though I do remember one carpet-biting rage when his father would not let him dig a hole in the flower bed. Also his open verbal anger against the first boarding-school headmaster. So all those questions in the diary, what if he did so and so, could he not be looking for my hidden anger? Then doesn't the blacked-out eye of the little man with the see-through house suggest he must not let himself know about all this in either of us?

The smashed windows

In connection with the picture of the stone-throwing woman, I now noticed the two star-shaped forms put in place of two of the windows, one of them over the window where Star slept. Since they are star-shaped, they could also stand for smashed windows, the result of stone-throwing. Surely there must have been much anger against Star for deserting him by having the accident.

However, looking back I had the idea that the sudden loss of Star was perhaps not quite as traumatic as might have been expected; or rather, that it had a good side, as well as the sense of loss. This was because I now remembered how strongly he had reacted when she had kept him on the reins too long when they were out for walks, preventing him from running freely. Was it not likely that she found it hard to let him grow out of babyhood to independence, since it was only babies that she knew about?

As for the staircases shown in the picture, I knew that, in general, staircases have rich symbolic significance. It is interesting that in J's picture, each attic room has its separate stairway, whereas in our actual house there was only one stairway to both the attic rooms. The second stair on the middle storey of the house is placed where his father had his work-bench, so I suspected there was again anger with the farmer-father.

The traditional religious use of the stairway symbol seems to come later when he puts carefully drawn ladders (of Jacob's Ladder dream?) on the lighthouses, while on top of each lighthouse is a cross.

The kittens' dead mother and the triumphant cat

My idea of the stone-throwing being really against me did fit in with the theme of the next story, since it is called "The Kittens," but tells of only one kitten, whose mother was dead, yet who lived at home, his house being "very comfortable." At the bottom of the same page is the drawing of the kitten with a tremendous flourish to its long tail and looking very pleased with itself. Opposite, in pencil, is a house again with three chimneys, but now only a little smoke, and both people and kittens at the upstairs windows. Also this house is now firmly on the ground with a garden and two garden paths, these making two rather breast- or buttock-like curves on each side of the garden gate. There is also a shadowy tree which is full of leaves.

Looking at these drawings, especially the triumphant flourish of the kitten's tail, I began to wonder whether the story of the dead mother did not in part mark J's final realisation that he did not have to die when I did; in fact, that he was a separate person, rooted in the ground of his own being, with an inner life of his own, full of his memories of people or parts of people or different parts of himself, all shown as faces and kittens looking out of the windows.

In fact, when faced with the dead mother story and its pictures, I now found myself needing to meditate on the question of what had actually happened in J's imaginative world, as a result of his having sent me, while I was in Spain, the chaotic picture letter with its "wrecked train," "terrible dragon," etc. (all quite unrecognisable as such). There was also the undoubted fact that apparently I had not taken any notice of it when I got home. So the question now arose, would the results of the wrecked train etc. still be there, in the form of the kitten's dead mother story? If so, the triumphant look in the cat's eyes (clearly no longer a kitten) could even stand not only for his delight in realising he did not have to die when I did, but also for the thought of getting his own back, paying me out for what had seemed like my not caring about his feelings at all, even betrayal of them. Also in the house picture (page 7) opposite the cat, with those two garden paths, might they not also stand for two opposite attitudes in him? I even thought, could the cat and the house stand for a bit of a swagger, part of him trying to claim he did not need me at all, he could manage quite nicely by himself, thank you?

Living in a wood

Next, it seemed likely that he was trying to tell how feelings of the precariousness of total dependence have led to the daydream of getting away from it all, finding a place of his own, surrounded by nature. Thus the next story says there was a boy who lived in a little house in a wood, the house being "very comfortable." Below (page 8) is a drawing of a little house in a wood, with a small armless figure, and what might be a cat or a dog. Opposite this (page 9) there is a big blue and red house, and now there are only two chimneys, both with big contraptions on top of them. But there is nobody looking out of the windows, which are half-covered by curtains. Here, I wondered whether he meant that however much fun it could be to be a separate person, there could also be some loneliness to be faced when there are no people at the windows. Actually one of the attic windows of the house is totally curtained off, as if for privacy – or secrecy – or darkness?

I also noticed that not only is this the first time the contraptions on the chimney tops appear, but also that one is in the form of a black and white grid, the other a kind of bitten-into moon shape. There is also a shadowy tree beside the house, but now it has no leaves.

The boat that rocked

Now comes the story called "The Boat," which says there was a man on the boat, which rocked and rocked and rocked. The man nearly fell off, but climbed back onto the boat.

Here the top three-quarters of the page is covered with blue chalk under the writing. At the bottom is a drawing of a small steamer with three people on it, two bigger and one smaller, and the word "cat" (page 10). Also there is a smaller boat with one person on it, and a straight column of steam.

I thought that perhaps the blue chalk here is more to do with water than with sky, with the dangers of being drowned. Also, could not the idea of the boat rocking be to do with the risks of being a separate person in danger of secretly rocking the boat in the father–mother–child triangle?

Having been let down

Some time after writing about the rocking boat, I remembered, with pain, how I had, very early in J's life, literally let him rock himself down. It was when Star was on her first holiday, and J was about 6 months old. We were staying with cousins in the country. On the first evening I had tucked him up in the Moses basket we had brought him in, and put it on a very low sofa while I went out of the room for a little while. What I did not realise was how energetically he could bounce himself around before sleeping. So when I came back I found he had bounced himself, cocooned in the basket and blankets, onto the floor. He did not seem upset, and after I had put him and the basket somewhere else, he went off to sleep quite easily. Only now did I come to wonder whether this memory could have appeared in the rocking boat story. On the following day, or soon after, we had taken some photos of him. Looking at them now, I could not help thinking there was a rather affronted look, even suppressed indignation. Was it at his having been let down, not properly held, just when he had been using his own muscles so enjoyably?

The fox's new house

After this, on the opposite page is a story called "The Fox" that again seems to mark some change in his inner life, since it says "the fox decided to change his house and the new house was very comfortable, the old house was very uncomfortable." There is no picture but the word "END" is written after the story, as if he feels he has come through something. Also there is a tiny figure inserted before the word "change." It was only after study of the later story, called "The Two Boats" (its picture is obviously associated with London's Tower Bridge across the Thames), that I came to guess that the fox's old home being "very uncomfortable" could very likely express, amongst other things, his growing awareness of the troubles, which were there but not openly expressed, in our marriage.

Living in a hollow tree

The following story (page 12) is actually called "The Boy and the Fox" (though the fox is not actually mentioned in the story) and says that the boy lived in a hollow tree which is again "very comfortable" and warm. There is a drawing at the bottom of a bit of tree-trunk with a hole in it, like a woodpecker's nesting place. But there is also a little house with a very big window just under its roof and beside it a scribbled tree, and animal of sorts (these last three at a rather cock-eyed angle to the ground).

By now it did seem to me that J was, in these drawings, trying to tell about aspects of the lifelong struggle to find what is truly one's own inner place to live from. In this connection, the hollow tree provides a strong containing space, safe from outside intruders and attackers, who are to be warded off: the tree has what look like very spiky leafless branches. But also, I felt, since trees are cylindrical, it could be that he was trying to find an image for the experience of coming to live inside one's own body, inhabit one's own body space, and therefore be able to be in touch with nature within, with the actual source of one's liveliness. Certainly the tree image has some advantages over the square house in that it is nearer the tubular shape of the upright human body. (Remember the blind man in the Bible who, when sight was returning, said he saw "men as trees walking.")

As for the cock-eyed angle of the little house, it might be just the result of his not really knowing how to portray a house on a hillside. On the whole, however, I thought that it was really meant to be cock-eyed, together with the big window under the roof. It might even be an attempt to depict his awareness of my own problem of still being deeply immersed in my school research job, thus living too much in my head, and liable to make things a bit cock-eyed for both of us, he being the little animal also on the hillside.

However this may be, I found myself being glad that he seemed to have felt about to take into himself something "Nice and warm and comfortable." Actually this capacity to find good emptiness in the hollowness of the tree did, for me, link up with what I had myself been driven to write about during the time in Spain when he sent the unanswered picture letter.

It now occurred to me that, by using the idea of living comfortably in a hollow tree, he might even be beginning to feel that darkness itself has its value; beginning to be able to accept not knowing, accept the mysteriousness of just being? Hence perhaps also the unspecified animal (cat or fox?). In any case, it seemed to me that his intuition, or what Willliam Blake called "each man's poetic genius," was at work here, providing him with metaphors with which to try to communicate with other selves, as well as with himself.

Blown off an engine

The next story (pages 13 and 14) introduces quite another theme, a container that can move – i.e. a train, and a train that was always going puff puff puff, and with a man sitting on the safety valve so that when the valve explodes, the man is blown off. However on the next page there is a drawing of an engine emitting two huge rushes of steam, but the man is not blown off, and is leaning comfortably against the safety valve. The puff puff of the train made me think of his father's breathing problems, with his use of an adrenaline spray. If so, what did the two great rushes of steam mean? Could it refer to his hearing – or his fears of hearing – his father and me having a quarrel? However the picture, with its nonchalant figure not blown off at all, but leaning against the top of the engine, suggests that if this fear existed it had been surmounted – or perhaps only denied? I had another thought when I noticed that there was a crown on the lolling figure's head. Could it possibly be that J was having an ironic thought – that between the bouts of asthma, his father was really having quite a nice life, in a lordly sort of way, not having to go to work at all but doing just what he liked.

Two boats, two lighthouses and a bridge

Following this is a much longer story, its drawings spread over nine pages, called "The Two Boats" (although the "Two" is spelt "Tow"). Accompanying the story is a large picture covering two pages, showing two lighthouses on each side of a river, linked by a bridge, which the story says is made of wire rope, with five lanterns hanging from it (pages 16 and 17). There are three boats under the bridge, one a steamer and two sailing boats, much smaller.

The story says that the boat has three people on it and one child, called Twink, who likes playing with the dog, Bobby Tink. The bit of the story above the picture says that Bobby Tink had tried to jump on to a passing lifeboat. Apparently he does not succeed, because we are soon told that he is playing with Twink on the lighthouse stairway.

Three people on a boat: surely this fitted in with his family situation, his father, me and Joyce, with himself as the child, while the dog may emphasise his maleness. The form of this first bridge picture, though obviously inspired by seeing London's Tower Bridge over the Thames, has been developed into the two lighthouses and the structure of these is entirely his own invention. But why has he chosen London Bridge for the form of the picture? Oh, yes, the nursery rhyme "London Bridge is falling down, falling down." But his bridge is made of a wire rope and has not fallen down. In general, then, it looks as if, amongst other things, he is struggling in the picture to reassure himself that our marriage was not in danger of breaking down.

However, the story and the picture are also likely to be saying many other things. For instance, why is the child called Twink? Oh yes, the nursery rhyme "Twinkle twinkle little star, How I wonder what you are …" Yes, of course, he is busy wondering who he is. But also, can there not be a twinkle in one's eye when one is not too solemn about something. Joyce certainly had one, though I doubt if Star had. There was also likely to be something else, as indicated by his choice of the image of lighthouses as well as boats, which is that lighthouses are there to protect. Thus the lighthouses and the lanterns joining them seemed appropriate symbols not only for parents, but also to mark a big step in his seven years of living, a step to do with mind becoming more aware of itself. Here I could not help remembering the arrival of Elihu in Blake's illustrations to the Book of Job, with the printed text saying "I am very young and ye are very old." In J's pictures and stories it was as if the primitive theme of violence and death of the wild thing in the fox and farmer story had given place to something quite different, to the two separate givers of light, linked by more lights (lanterns). No longer are there traps that one could blindly fall into in the dark, but what could be a new kind of awareness of what it means to be human.

The idea of a big step in growth reminded me also that, according to two date markings by a teacher, the stories were probably written once a week. So, although my guess was that they were written during a period of a number of weeks, I felt there could be a big historical time gap in the themes, since he begins the first three of them, and only those, with the standard fairy-tale beginning "Once upon a time ..." almost as if these stories' themes belonged to himself when younger.

Further, I notice that there are some very special things about these lighthouses. Each one is topped with a squared platform with railings and a little tower in the centre carrying something like a small church steeple, usually with a cross on top. In the first bridge picture both are shown reached by many ladders though the one on the right is only coloured in red, with blue curtains, by contrast with the left-hand one which is lovingly drawn in red, blue and green. Also the word "wet" is written twice near the various boats, and "sand" written twice in the foreground, which is coloured yellow. The steamer has a rectangular structure on its mast, with four black balls, two at each end; it looks like some sort of aerial. Also there is a straight column of steam reaching right up to near the edge of the paper, suggesting a quiet wind-free day, and quite unlike the turmoil of black smoke from the house in the first picture.

Furthermore, the two lighthouses are not identical in shape: the one on the left is tall and narrow, the one on the right more squat, but mounted on what looks like a large dark cliff or rock. Certainly this difference could introduce the themes of male and female, mother and father, in which case the lanterns could be to do with a preoccupation about communication between them. So, in so far as he could be trying to tell something about the light of consciousness, his own and other people's, then the lanterns could even be to do with communicating by words, words as sources of meaning, of light, strung along a thread of grammatical or poetical coherence, as against chaotic disorder. Thus the picture could surely also be about how far he himself can imaginatively allow his parents to have a creative relation to each other, as well as to do with the need to communicate with the male and female sides of himself. In short, it seems to be a picture of many forces felt to be at work within himself as well as indicating something of what he was aware of in the family situation.

Different levels of meaning

During all this time, I had been thinking what an apt symbol a house, or a lighthouse, is for one's own body-mind self-awareness, since it allows for different meanings on different levels, or storeys. On the level of sensation, the ground level of bodily experience, the lighthouse on the left surely does stand for his father as a bodily presence, shown as male by the very phallic protuberance over the river with a little man on it; while the other lighthouse, the smaller one on the rock, has two protuberances, one on each side, but no little figures standing on them. Also, in the second bridge picture (page 23) the cross on top of the father lighthouse has apparently turned into a weather vane, perhaps something to make sure which way the winds of his parents' moods blow? Also on top of the lighthouse is a quite clear drawing of a cock – safely out of reach of foxes.

The tides and the crescent moon

It is in the second bridge picture that he has once more felt
the need to break out into verbal symbols, for the words "wet"
and "sand" appear again in the foreground and background
of the river. Also there is a tiny sailing boat near the steamer,
which looks as if it is anchored to a buoy (boy?).

Here I thought that J had been fascinated, as I too
had always been, when walking over the bridges to see the
tidal aspect of the Thames, the daily influence of the moon
penetrating into the very heart of London, creating the
recurrently covered stretch of sand (or mud) between the
water and the shore. In fact there is a contraption on top of
the lantern that is itself directly above the steamboat in the
lighthouse picture that does have, once more, in a slightly
blurred way, the shape of a crescent moon.

The lighthouse keeper's finished task?

The next stage of the story (page 18) describes how the
lighthouse keeper was putting five new wicks in the oil
lamps and ten new candles in the lanterns. Underneath are
drawings: first, on the extreme left, the lighthouse keeper
is on the ground carrying two lanterns, one in each hand,
with two more beside him; and the drawing is divided into
three sections. In the middle section there are five lanterns,
all of unequal size, and a single lighthouse with only its top
half shown, much less lovingly drawn, and with no ladders
to reach it. It is also in red and blue chalk and has a cross
on top. On the other page is a repeat of this one, but now
there are two of them, again joined by a wire rope with five
lanterns hanging from it; but these two lighthouses have no
crosses on top of their spires. The story above this picture
says the lighthouse keeper had finished putting all the new
wicks and candles in the lanterns. I thought, just what has J
finished? Is it perhaps learning the basic rules of grammar
and spelling? However, the odd thing about this picture is
that the handles of the lanterns, shown as circles, make
them look like the heads of little figures, so that in the third
section of the picture, what he calls lanterns almost look

like wrapped-up dead babies hung there. Of course, in the diary he had talked of his wolf going to fetch a brother or a sister, but he had had to face the fact that he himself had no womb so could never have live babies coming out of himself; or, as he had once put it, his chicks were not real chicks, they would never grow up. Certainly he had to face the sorrow, mourning for those never-to-be-born-out-of-himself, as well as the fact of having no brothers and sisters. However, in the first half of the picture the lanterns are carefully tended and all of different sizes, again almost like words in a sentence.

Playing on the dark stairway

The story continues to tell how Bobby Tink and Twink were playing on the lighthouse stairs where lamps were lit because the stars were always dark. It says that Bobby Tink was having a lovely time when one of the lamps blew out and Twink came and lit it again. Underneath is a pencil drawing of a very dark spiral stairway, the spiral going from left to right (page 21). I found that my first involuntary thought was "the bright day is done and we are for the dark." And the second was to do with the diary notes, where he cheerfully tells his father and me about how "Albert" (his penis) liked to be played with. Then the light going out could even indicate a rush of anxiety about the sensory pleasure in this, getting mixed up with the aggressive imaginings towards his father that are recorded in one or two places in the diary. (Including the theme of the fox killing the farmer's cock.) If so, then the light going out might mean he did not want to know that, in the magic of his omnipotent thinking, he could have felt his fox killing the farmer's cock had led to such barrenness – no more babies after him. But it is Twink himself who relights the lanterns.

Aspects of nest building

Such thoughts took me back over the whole diary, especially the time J said he thought he had been born without a penis; also his so frequent play of making nests, containers for new life. Although it could be that he was here expressing the fact that he knew about the existence of womb envy (even if Freud did not), the longing to give birth out of his own body could also mean that the aggression, if that was what it was, that could partly have produced the dead mother story, could also be seen on the level of competition for his father's love, which could then lead to imaginatively getting rid of me as a rival. (In fact, the inverse of Freud's Oedipus conflict.) At the same time I kept thinking that the nest building must also have to do with his feeling about all the times when I seemed to be not properly holding him: in my reveries, or too busy with my work. But also all the making of nests could have other meanings, such as a wish to get back, imaginatively, to the unity of the womb state, in order to have a fresh start; to be re-born into finding his own containment and boundary, his independent self, inhabiting his own body, and freed from anxieties about what his fox self had imaginatively done. Whatever the possible relevance of such an idea, I felt that the real culmination of all the nest building was the story book itself, a self-created container for his growing awareness of his separate and unique identity.

Avoiding rivalry with father

There was also the bit in the story about the dog trying to jump off the steamer onto a passing lifeboat. Surely this could be another way of expressing a wish he had been born a girl, for that could mean he need no longer be in a dangerous rivalry with a farmer-father who sets traps for foxes. This idea seems to be depicted in terms of the life-saving boat, but obviously only as a passing idea, since on the next page, Bobby Tink is back on the steamboat.

Playing dominoes, accepted rivalry

The story continues, telling how Twink and three people were playing dominoes on the ship, and "the lighthouse keeper asked if he could join in the game, and Twink said he could. The people thought it was great fun." Underneath is another picture of the first lighthouse, still in red, green and blue chalk, and even more lovingly drawn (page 23). The steamboat is still there, but this picture does not include the smaller lighthouse on its rock on the far side of the bridge. Does this perhaps mean that he has now settled for the fact of being a boy?

This second lighthouse and bridge picture, with the addition about the lighthouse keeper coming to play dominoes with them (I doubt if his father really did play dominoes with him), does include another idea – that there is something beyond the immediate family circle, i.e. the "people" who approve of the game. They are presumably thinking it is all right to have fun, in spite of all the family problems.

Having his own tent

Now comes a quite different story, about a caravan that only went five miles at a time, and the three-acre field it was in (pages 24 to 27). I remembered that I had actually bought an old horse-type caravan that year, in order to have a little foothold in the country. I doubt if J had actually seen it when he wrote the story, but it tells how the boy in the caravan thought it great fun to make a hut in the ditch. There are two big drawings of the caravan, each different, (pages 25 and 26), and opposite the second is a tent with a tree beside it, and another very small tent. Inside are two tables or seats, and a little grinning man, with upstanding hair, very solid feet, but no arms. The tent has its own flag, with a red and blue diagonal cross on it. On the horizon of the field (the first time there has been a horizon in his pictures) there is another tent with what looks like two people in it, also a small house all coloured blue, but with five windows, each indicated by a cross in red chalk. On the right is another steamer in blue chalk with plenty of smoke. I thought that these items were expressing his joy in the idea of freedom to mark out and take possession of his own living space – now set wherever he pleased, even, as the story says, in a ditch – and that it would be fun.

The goods train

There follows the story, which has no title, about the goods train that went 104 miles each day and carried mostly coal and oil (page 28). There is a pencil drawing of the train and its driver, so now it seems that from the fun of the hut in a ditch, he moves to the idea of work to convey necessary goods, as well as developing further the theme of numbers which has already been present in the diary. But there is also a concern with the idea of measuring speed, and of regularity, both ways of helping one to tolerate the basic uncertainties of living. Thus the next story, again with no title, returns to the theme of bridges, telling how buses go over Westminster and Battersea bridges three and four times a day. There is a rough pencil drawing of a bridge (not the Tower Bridge of the Two Boats picture) with no water underneath.

The station and the porter

Following this are six pages of a long story (without a title) about a porter who lived at a station hotel, which is carefully drawn in pencil and blue chalk, with realistic details of advertisements, a slot machine, and three chimneys, each surmounted by a very complicated contraption, presumably still anti-smoke devices, but more ingenious than the earlier ones (page 30). There are also five gas lamps, each having a chain to pull them on. Again there is a bridge shape, now obviously over the railway line, and holding two big lamps (page 31). The story tells about the porter's daily duties from 5 a.m. – putting water in all the engines, cleaning out the boilers, turning on the gas lamps and making up the waiting-room fire; also helping passengers to get off incoming trains. At the bottom of the page is a little man shown with arms outspread, one hand white and the other black, the whole figure in the form of a cross.

The black hand and the white hand

I found this story of the devoted porter looking after everything and everybody especially interesting in the light of some of the diary entries. Here he is cleaning out and putting water in the engines, and this seemed to me that he was perhaps making amends for the idea, described in the diary, of dirtying his father with faeces and laughing triumphantly. So the little man at the bottom of the page, with one white and one black hand outstretched, seemed to be marking the possibility of being able to bridge the gap between loving and hating his father, accepting that both feelings are part of himself. Also, this seemed to mark an idea of getting rid of the defensive denial, shown in the diary, about the Anglican service with its prayer of General Confession; J had said there was nothing he felt sorry about.

On the next page (page 34) comes the addition that the porter's job of helping the passengers off when the train came in was because the steps were rather high, but when one day an express arrived, he did not have to because the train step was lower. The story adds that when he had no other jobs to do, he used to sit in the cloakroom. Here I wondered, does the cloakroom mean something hidden? Was this yet another way of avoiding having to face the rivalry with his father that he had been able to be open about in his earlier years? The bit about the lower step is in fact the end of the porter story, except for two tiny houses, in pencil, at the bottom of the page.

And what about the station hotel itself? It is certainly a special kind of house to do with travel and moving on. As for the so helpful porter, I wondered just who he is; possibly one of J's ideals for himself, what some part of him feels he ought to be like?

Also, since the story does say that when an express train came he did not have to help the passengers get down, it could mean his wish for parents who did not need so much help from him, through his being the so good child (porter). But also, on another level, it could be a useful metaphor for his becoming aware of, perhaps quite suddenly ("one day"), the two different kinds of thinking, the slow process of the logical discursive kind and the quick flashes of intuitive thinking that does not have to stop at all the stations on the way.

The end house and the semi-detached one

This one, in contrast to the earlier uncoloured house of page 7, with its three chimneys, its windows showing people and kittens, and opposite the cat with the curly tail, is the house labelled "The End," also uncoloured (page 36). Not only does this have five plain chimneys, suggesting perhaps the five days of week at school and also my five days a week at work, there is also, beside and attached to it, another tiny one, but with its own chimney and column of smoke.

This suggested that the earlier house, seemingly in its own grounds and opposite the triumphant cat, was not only a bit of denied pain but also a pipe dream for the future, since, for the present, he had to face the fact that he was still a 7-year-old quite dependent on his parents. Of course there could also be a deeper internal meaning, a sense that part of him had not yet entirely accepted the day in the diary when he had tried to use my hand to feed himself instead of his own.

Fitting in with this idea was the fact that on the last page of the porter story, at the bottom, there are these two tiny houses, looking as if they had been semi-detached, but the other half is missing. The one on the right, which is the more carefully drawn, creates rather a forlorn effect, just because the half it should be attached to simply is not there. Thus, although it seemed to me he had earlier, opposite the curly-tailed cat picture, depicted an exciting moment of realising he was separate and need not die when I did, there was also a hard fact to accept – that there must be a sense of loss in being separate. Again, however, there is a contrast; the joyfully grinning little man in his own tent in the second caravan picture had suggested a growing capacity to achieve and enjoy his own separate identity. And this contrasts with the fact that most of the little men have no feet.

Having thus had first thoughts on J's book, I tried now to summarise the results. There came a growing sense of a thread developing through all the stories to do with the idea of survival, of somehow transcending the first grim fairytale-like story of anger, violence, killing and retaliation. So, in a see-through house, he does seem to reach a new kind of awareness, in spite of showing one crossed-out eye in the little man on the ground floor. There is certainly a depiction of the immense complexity of being human, all shown by the different levels linked by staircases. Even the little man with one eye crossed out did produce, for me, an echo of my own experience in Spain, something that I had taken so long to know how to begin to understand for ordinary living.

And then his getting his own house in a wood suggested the idea of comfort in just being, being in his own body and valuing stillness, but also able to move about as shown in the nearby little man with his unspecified animal (fox, cat or dog). Also in the book there soon begin to be boats, trains, and buses as centrepieces for the different stories, which then lead on to the questions of speed, rhythms of buses over bridges, regularity, predictability; for, after all, nothing dreadful has happened from the explosion of steam from one of the trains. And then the whole theme of bridges turns up, the bridging of opposites of all kinds, contraries; including comfort as well as danger. And in the end having his own tent, even with a bit of defiance in it, claiming the right to pitch it in a ditch if he chooses, just for the fun of it. So now he can afford to be, at least for a time, the helpful porter. The smashed windows in the see-through house could also be seen as stars, as givers of light.

It was here that I remembered the kind of tree or chart of levels of experience that I had made use of in the schools research; it was lurking at the back of my mind, and helped me to sort out what use I could make of J's stories and pictures on the different levels. Thus it was that after remembering this chart I noticed on the ground floor of the see-through house and on the opposite side of the little man there is what looks like a store of logs (coloured brown) suggesting an available source of inner warmth? Also now I thought the little man's mouth was not quite as grim as I had first thought, and I noticed that in the second half of the book, after the explosion of steam, a dominant theme is light (lanterns, candles, lighthouses), surely a move towards recognising awareness as a central value.

There is one aspect of the Station Hotel picture that I found especially important: the use J has made of the space on top of the chimneys, which he has for inventions of his own.

PART FOUR

Towards a change of aim

4

Crosses, trees and no arms or feet

J's little man with feet

After this last chapter showing attempts to see if I could get an idea of what it might have been that J was struggling to say, I began to have an inkling that my purpose in writing about his story book, and the diary, was changing. Having started out, as I have said, intending to seek publication philanthropically, for the benefit of other parents, wanting to show how much a 7-year-old can know, in metaphoric terms, about the joys and sorrows of his childhood, I now had to ask myself, again, whether his story of the kitten whose mother was dead might be not only an idea growing from his anger at the ways in which I had failed him, by going to Spain; it could also be something he felt about me, something that I did not then know in myself. Nevertheless, in spite of the hint of a change in my task, I went on trying to understand his communications, mainly in terms of what else he could have been trying to say by writing the book. Only now and then could I glimpse the ways in which I would have to use his images for my own needs for more self-awareness; in short, it was after growing misgivings that what I had been writing looked like an attempt to analyse my own son, that I suddenly thought, "No, it's his images analysing me, helping me to find out what had been left out of my own couch analysis."

The cross and the bitten-into moon

The first of J's images that I now found myself having to deal with on many levels was the form of the cross that he had so often used in various ways. There were many questions to ask.

Did it mean he was thinking about the Christian use of it, and concerned with the crucifixion? Certainly, as far as I knew, he had had no religious indoctrination; none of the people who had looked after him were church-goers and the school he had been going to was quite undenominational. Of course, according to the diary, I had read to him out of a picture book called *The Childhood of Jesus*, and there had been that frequent game of making "cathedrals" out of bits of dead wood. In addition there was what looks like a crescent moon on one of the chimney-pots of the Station Hotel. This now reminds me that there had been a remark in his diary about wanting to see the whole moon and asking what had "taken a bit out of it." Also his saying, aged 2¾, "I mustn't bite you, no, only taste you." I even remembered how, when breastfeeding him after he had got his first tooth, I had suddenly jumped out of my skin in sheer surprise at the needle-sharp pain, so totally unexpected, and how he never bit me again, although I had never said, "don't."

Since this brings in the idea of physical pain, either given or received, could it not be that J was using the cross, on one level, as a symbol for his experience of and ideas about pain and fears of dying?

The use of the red cross

I now noticed there was certainly another aspect of his use of the form of the cross, for I saw that in the lighthouses built on a rock, which I had been thinking of as the female one, there was red chalk as well as black pencil on the cross; also that he had used red chalk on those pencil crosses that indicated windows in the little house shown on the horizon in the second caravan picture. Might it be that this belongs to its conventional meaning, the Red Cross that stands for compassion, aid for those injured in war, etc.? The fact that this little house is on the horizon, together with a steamer and a little tent with two people in it, could mean that he was wondering about his future, what he will be when he is a man: perhaps go to sea, hopefully find the mate that he had talked about in the diary, and perhaps even do work for people in trouble, actually tend wounds and, symbolically, mend both those he had hurt in imagination and also the hurt he himself had suffered.

But could all this apply to me?

One answer came when I remembered there was this other quite different use of the word cross as applied to the grumpy woman in one story who threw stones. When wondering again about her, I came back to the odd fact that there are no other women in the story book, shown as such; could it even be that neither he nor I had then really faced the stone-thrower in ourselves, though maybe he had done so more than I, since he had at least drawn a house with what could partly be seen as having smashed windows.

Crosses, trees and body awareness

Yet another aspect of the cross, or related to it, was the fact that in several of the pictures that show a house, there is also a tree, once even a whole wood of them. The idea of a live tree, with its roots hidden in darkness and its branches outspread in the light, seemed to me an apt symbol for a way in which one can experience one's body–mind existence, once having learnt to stand upright. Further, in my own body awareness I had often thought of how this verticality is counter-balanced by the horizontal line of one's shoulders. Hence also an association with the wood from a dead tree used for crucifixion, a kind of cruelty in which the pull of gravity has been transferred to the nails in the hands and the feet, away from the natural foot contact with Mother Earth.

Having no arms

My next query, related to this, was why nearly all the little men in the pictures have no arms. Seeking an answer

I now remembered how when he and I first came home from the hospital where J was born, he was neatly pinned up in a shawl, and how I had gone on with it because he seemed to like it. For instance, one night in the early weeks, having been woken by his crying, I had put out a hand in the dark, to his cot beside the bed, and felt feather-soft fingers waving in the air. When I got out and wrapped him up again he fell asleep at once, but I had gone on doing it too long, as a friend later pointed out. Now I wondered, could some sort of memory of an over-long constriction of his arms be appearing in the drawings? Or could it be that there was some sort of anxiety about masturbation being expressed? Against this last idea, I remembered how in the diary he had so gaily told about how his "Albert" liked to be stroked. There had seemed to be no guilt about it, and he had certainly never been told not to do it. However, later in the diary there had appeared the idea of lying on top of me. So could it possibly be that it was guilt about ideas of attacking his father as a rival, combined with the phallic enjoyment of his own body, that had led to the obliteration of the arms of the little men? All except the man from the lighthouse while tending the lanterns, and the little figure under the story of the porter who devotedly cleans up the engines.

This last idea now took me back to the very first story in the book, to the house above the drawing of the fox that killed the farmer's cock, and the fact that the house with all its black smoke is itself only three-quarters black, the rest a lovely rosy red. If the house is himself, and if the black smoke is showing him to be full of angry fires, then perhaps the blackness of three-quarters of the house could have a further meaning, in terms of the darkness of sorrow for what his fox self had done. Then the rosy red could suggest some hope for a happier solution for the rivalry with his father? The fact that the house has a clearly-marked side garden gate implies that you could get round to see the back, that the front is not all there is. Which surely suggests, on one level, an urge to wholeness of self-perception? If so, did the constant variations on the cross symbol mean that his pictorial metaphoric ability was leading him to the truth that there is no healthy escape from the agonising experience of both loving, longing to preserve, and at times wanting to hurt or even get rid of the same person? This idea would certainly fit in with the theme of the dog in one of the bridge stories, Bobby Tink, and Twink playing on the dark stairs and the light going out (story book, pages 21 to 22); which could indicate a momentary obliterating of ideas too mixed with conflict between loving and hating. Also this would in fact make sense of the next bit of the story, when the lighthouse keeper actually asks to come and join the game of dominoes, that is, a shared game of open rivalry with father, that society approves of ("The people thought it was great fun"). Thus the lighthouse keeper is now far from the retaliating farmer who set a trap for the fox that killed his cock.

The cross and the black and white hands

The form of the cross turns up, yet again, in a less conventional way, in the cross-like structure of the three lighthouses between which hang the little lanterns that, at first, I thought suggested babies; and here the man filling these lanterns does have arms. So, could not these lantern-like shapes needing to be filled indicate J's wish for a potent restored father, so that there could be live babies after him – or at least the brother that the diary says his wolf was going to fetch.

The other drawing where the little man has arms, the one under the porter story, is actually in the shape of a cross, his arms being outstretched, with one white and one black hand. And here I thought the widespread arms did give a feeling of hope, of openness to all experience. The light and the dark, the white and the black, as if realising the contraries that have to be faced: joy and sorrow, love and hate, compliance and defiance, etc. And what joins these in this last drawing is the little man's body, the place where opposites have to come together, relate to each other, become reconciled and transformed, i.e. in the human heart.

My father's dream

Another idea that was coming up again was about the great strong hooks in the caravan pictures. Could it possibly be that J's wolf had told him something that it had actually taken me thirty years to discover, then many more years to find out how to make full use of it, i.e. the discovery that of attending to and feeling the full weight of one's limbs, especially one's hands and arms, did provide a strong sense of be-ingness? I remembered vividly my delighted shock when first discovering this, in Santa Fe in America. But why the years of difficulty in learning how to use this discovery in a daily way? Suddenly there came a surprising hint of a possible answer. I remembered that the only dream of his that my father ever described to me, with much mirth, was that if he moved his arms they would fall off! Of course, when he said this, it only made me laugh. I now wondered, what does it mean, arms that drop off? What also does in fact drop off from one's body? Of course, it's faeces from one's bowels. Only now did it occur to me to wonder whether, by drawing so many armless little men, J might not, amongst other things, have been struggling with a left-over infantile problem of confusing the movement of one's bowels and movement of one's arms and hands (i.e. doing something).

Or could this be just my problem? Certainly I had to wonder whether J's drawings of so many armless little men might not be to do with an undoubted fact, that in spite of many years spent lying on the psychoanalytic couch, and plenty of physiotherapy, I had not managed to cure myself of hunching my left shoulder and thus producing a tension which did prevent me from feeling the full weight of my arm. This happened especially whenever I was doing practical tasks at shoulder level, a hunching which always led to a mid-back pain and the need to lie down flat on my back, totally "given" to gravity.

Images for his experience of gravity and energy

Such thoughts took me on to the fact of J's obvious interest in gravity, all those hanging lanterns and the two containers hanging from hooks in the caravan pictures. What were they meant to be? They certainly look like containers of some sort. Anyway, firmly defying gravity by means of those strong hooks. And the thought of escaping gravity reminded me of, many years before, seeing J making his first attempt to climb the bottom step of the stairway from the nursery, and how he was dead white in his determination to do it. Ideas about his experience of his own weight now brought me to consider what he might be saying about his experience of other forces, those sources of goodness that he had represented by the goods train carrying oil and coal, the lighthouse keeper carrying oil for the lanterns, or the porter making up the waiting-room fire. Of course all these raw substances are sources of energy, but they have to have something done to them, somebody has to act deliberately and purposefully if the substances are to be of any use, work has to be done, as the driver of the goods train is doing, and in the later story, the busy porter, who has to use his arms, not only to bear weights of people's baggage but also to help some of the passengers down off the train.

Having no feet

There was also the fact that most of the figures not only have no arms, but except for the gay little one in the tent in the second caravan picture, they have no feet. It was after thinking about this when still trying to sort out my papers that I came across an early drawing by J, when he was 3½, six months before the angry "picture letter." To me it was quite clearly a person, quite unlike the unrecognisable scrawls of the picture letter, and it does have feet, large ones with long toes, although no hands, also a clearly marked navel, which he himself had drawn my attention to, hence my own scribbled note next to the drawing.

Whooping cough and losing his feet?

Naturally I now asked myself why he had lost his feet imaginatively during the three and a half years before

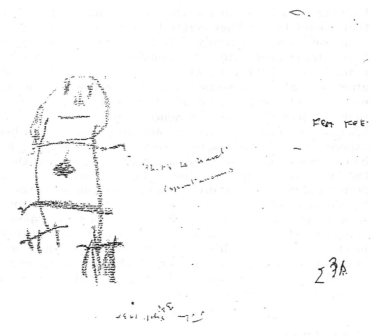

Those splendid feet

writing the story book, at age 7. I thought that the obvious way to seek an answer was to have another look at the diary. I found something I had quite forgotten, i.e. that he had had whooping cough rather badly that summer. The exact dates are not given, but it was almost certainly after he had made the drawing of the little man with such splendid feet. And the diary notes that he seemed, after the whooping cough, to have lost some of his "bounce." Certainly it was his first illness, and a distressing one. Was it not likely that the physical symptoms were felt by him as a kind of betrayal by his body, that up to now had often been such a joy to him? Could it be that it was this that had sent him back from accepted separateness, standing on his own feet, to the memory of a containing oneness, something he had once experienced as a reality, hence the navel that he had so carefully emphasised in the drawing? Perhaps strengthening this possibility is the fact that it was in November of that same year that he told me he would die when I did, i.e. that he feels he has no separate feet of his own.

The image of steam

Next, rather than the downward pull that those so strong hooks are defending against, the pull of gravity, the pull of Mother Earth, I found myself asking questions about an opposite force, something that goes up. For instance, all that smoke and steam from the chimneys, sometimes shown as a violent blackness, as in the farmer-fox story, but once shown going calmly straight up, almost reaching to the edge of the paper, as in the drawing of the boat in the first bridge picture. But sometimes feared, as if a safety valve had been sat on (story book, page 13) and a man blown off. Certainly we do use many ordinary metaphors to do with steam – "letting it off." "running out of it." being "all steamed up" – all to do with the fires of feeling.

Then was this not-blown-off safety-valve picture perhaps showing a time when he himself had exploded with anger, and nothing awful had happened? Or, as there are two columns of steam on the engine picture, had he perhaps heard his father and me having one of our rare rows, but had realised that it had not been a total disaster? Or could it even be to do with his 4-year-old inner explosion of rage at my being away in Spain, the one that had produced the wrecked-train drawing three years before, including what he had called "such a terrible dragon"? Could it be that my having come home safely had shown him that his terrible dragon of steam was not really so powerful after all, as no one gets blown off?

However, there was still the dead mother in the earlier story, so could it be that a partially dead mother – me – was still there, in his inner world; maybe still there just because I had not talked to him about the anger in his picture letter, not even recognised it? In which case the strong hooks defending against gravity could also be felt necessary to defend himself against the downward pull of depression, self-accusations for the recurrently imagined but not fully acknowledged ideas of killing me, ideas which he did come to accept openly later on in the diary.

J's God

Going back to the idea of no feet to support him – i.e. the lack of contact with the ground, of a separate bodily relation to Mother Earth – I now thought I had to face questions about his use of the word God. I had been brought up in an Anglican church-going family, but around the age of 6 had been upset by the Athanasian Creed, which, as I remembered it, says that whoever does not believe in what it says about Jesus will be damned. I had thought then, what about all those who have never heard of Jesus? I had been very worried by this, until years later, nearly adult, I had happened on William Blake's aphorism, "All religions are different manifestations of each nation's poetic genius." This then raised the problem of there being so many people, all over the world, continually insisting that their version of the "truth" is the only one and that other people must be made to believe it too, even killed if they don't agree. In this context I had been continually weighed down by thoughts of countless fatherless children and husbandless wives, resulting from all the wars growing from such literalness of beliefs. Certainly, in the 1930s, at the time of keeping the J diary, I had not sufficiently clarified my ideas on all this, so had not talked about it with him, but left it with his own statements that "It's God that makes him grow," that God knows things that he doesn't, and that it's God that looks after people.

J's wolf

Though there was not much discussion about God, there was plenty said about his wolf; so now came the question, what does his wolf mean to him? I thought he seemed to be using this word as a convenient name for various capacities in himself, as an actor playing many parts; thus his wolf is all colours, as if illustrating a growing awareness of the many aspects of his own self. Sometimes it can be his intuition, since his wolf "tells him things"; sometimes it is his longing not to be an only child, as when it "has gone to fetch a brother, no, a sister"; sometimes it is his wish to avoid conflict, as when it goes to stop the war in Spain, or to Canada (?) to shoot Mussolini, and "put him in a stew pot and eat him." This stew pot aspect of the wolf's tasks suggested that J's intuition could be telling him that his own aggressive wishes must be dealt with, not by projecting them into alligators etc., but by digesting them.

But what does his wolf eat? Sometimes J says it is flowers, such as lavender and grape hyacinths. I thought, what lovely words, could it be that J was talking about the joys, not only of smell, but also of certain words in one's mouth – for hyacinth is a most tasty word, most grape-like. But in another place he says his wolf only eats dead flowers. Can this perhaps express the intrusive thought that when a hyacinth is eaten it is no longer the same, no longer recognisably a hyacinth? Hence perhaps the reason why the wolf only eats dead plants, for then he is not responsible for killing them? But next comes the question, "Do wolves eat people?" Is J here struggling with having to accept the fact that one aspect of the urge to join up with what one loves is the wish to eat it, just as an infant tries to put everything it likes into its mouth?

Noticeably, his wolf is nearly always in some way active, even when he is said to be sitting in our pear tree. The pear tree does provide food for us, so this could be expressing his wish to be able to feed others from his own body, i.e. another example of the longing for motherhood that is shown in the diary – his preoccupation with what will hatch out of him. But what had actually hatched out of him was "The Story Book," something that will eventually feed its readers. So also, when in the diary he says he has just taken his wolf up for a talk with Daddy, was he not trying to be sure of his maleness, give up hankering for actual motherhood?

Another interesting question was what was the relation between his wolf and his chicks? I remembered that once he had said his wolf had gone to the seaside to fetch them back, using a steamroller – something powerful and capable of crushing. Also his chicks at one time seem to be like well-behaved children, as when he tells a family friend that they will come and look after her kitten for her when she is away. But on a quite different level I found myself thinking of them as wandering thoughts, absent-mindedness, often needing a massive steamroller effort of will to bring them back to the task in hand – for example, doing his school work. But also, since a steamroller has a very crushing power, used to make a road smooth and even, no bumps on its surface, it also seemed an apt metaphor for crushing impulses or ideas that might lead to emotional upheavals. I was now very well aware that such a steamroller could still be at work inside me, even though much modified by the years on the psychoanalytic couch.

A further aspect of his wolf seemed to be curiosity, as is indicated when he insisted that I come and see the dark end of the tunnel on the Heath where the stream comes out, saying that this is where his wolf goes in. Was it not that by seeing it, I had to sanction the erotic aspect of the wolf's wishes, as well as curiosity about all that is inside bodies?

Awe and the black dog

And what about the very early diary account of J circling round the black dog, making chanting noises? Just what could have been the feeling that he was expressing in quite so dramatic a way? Then I remembered the photo taken later of him and his little girl-friend parading round the garden holding their potties proudly in front of them. Could it possibly be that the black dog, being so intensely alive, played into the area of his early speculations about what it could really be that came out of his body, this something that was treated with such disrespect by the grown-ups, thrown down the lavatory? Could it be that he felt this dog was what he had made, and that it was alive and beautiful? I remembered too that there had seemed to be a kind of awe in his behaviour, in this circling round making chanting sounds, feelings of the kind that would perhaps later come to be spoken of as to do with the word sacred?

Or could it be just that he wanted to touch the dog but was afraid to?

J's feeling about deadness

Ideas of early infantile needs to confront the deadness of faeces now took me back to his ideas about death and dying. In the diary there was a bit about dying when I did, but also about the death of all Mr Brown's pigs, which he had loved so much; and later his saying that he himself was "not going to get dead." I even thought the death of Mr Brown's pigs could have appeared in one of J's few dreams that were told to me, the one in which "something rather nasty had happened" though he could not tell me just what it was. The same word "nasty" had appeared in another dream, saying there were some bird faeces in his bedroom which was rather nasty. This use of the word here suggested again the shock there could be on first discovering that what drops out of one's body is not alive, but just dead stuff to be thrown away. However, I also thought that J must have managed to deal creatively with this shock through the gradual discovery that he could learn to make meaningful marks on paper, marks which in the end had become the story book, something live enough to make a bridge of communication both with other people and with hidden parts of himself.

This idea seemed the more likely to be useful because, when preparing this book, I had one day been invited to a series of once-a-week evenings of play with paint or clay and had chosen clay which I had hardly ever used before. What had emerged, one on each evening, was a very expressive head, quite unplanned for, but each time, in beginning to work on it, I had felt certain nothing would emerge but a turd shape.

Something dead inside me?

Such thoughts now led me back again to the story of the kitten whose mother was dead, a theme that I seemed to have been constantly avoiding, I found myself wondering whether the story could have been due not only to my many absences and the angry ideas expressed in the "wrecked train" and the "terrible dragon" of his picture letter, when surely he could have felt that he had killed me in his imagination? But then I was alive enough to be told about it (cf. "Mind you tell Mummy!"). Could it not also be that he was trying to convey a feeling of something intermittently not sufficiently alive in me? This was painful to think about, but I did now have to face the fact that during some of those years there had certainly been a backdrop of anxiety about the security of our marriage, a preoccupation that could have been recurrently interfering with my sensitivity to his feelings, on a deep level. I knew that I had been, in general, keeping going the external expressions of love and concern for him, an awareness of which is perhaps implied in his repeated statement that the kitten whose mother was dead "lived in a very comfortable house." In fact I now suspected that he had been in some way aware that I was myself managing to keep dead my own doubts about the possibility of making the marriage work. In this connection perhaps even the strange rectangular shape on the top of the steamer in the first bridge picture, with its two pairs of black spots, although perhaps intended to be an aerial, could also be indicating the experience of two people in eye contact, something he might have wanted and not had enough of, owing to my own need to hide some of my anxieties, even from myself.

I now saw J's book as not only showing all the work that had been done both by his teachers and by himself, learning such things as the shapes of the sounds of the alphabet and how to write them, also how words are spelt and the right grammatical order if they are to make sense. It also shows his capacity both to create and play with images of his own experience, including images for his feelings, conflicts, fears and enjoyment, all embodied in the stories he told himself, the story-telling in fact a loving gift of himself made by the integrating of work and play, the love shown in the care taken to produce what is obviously meant to be read, with its carefully numbered pages and beautifully painted cover.

Actually, since his book had been lying unfound in our London house, he had had to wait for more than fifty years for its quality as a gift to be recognised. Perhaps too this way of seeing it provided a hint as to the meaning of two otherwise puzzling bits in the porter's story, how he had the job of making up the fire in the waiting room and also used sometimes to sit in the cloakroom, since station cloakrooms are places where baggage is left for safe keeping, to be collected at a later date. So it looked as if he could have been saying that he knew there were bits of himself that would have to wait, if they were to be recognised, either by himself or by all of us, some bits that perhaps had better be "cloaked," hidden away, at least for the time being.

And did he not also feel he might have to have had the task of stoking up the fire in order to combat my unadmitted depressive feelings about holding together the security of our marriage?

5

Water, tears and a use of gravity

By now I was quite certain that my aim in writing this book was changing. Having already tried to see what J's chimney-pot inventions might be saying for him I did not really know how to use this for myself. However, I came to see that the images I had used in earlier writings and had come to call "beads" must be once more looked at. Most especially, if I did not know where they were going I must keep my eyes skinned to spot them. In fact I thought I could now see what some dreams I had been having over the last few years might be about.

I had been rather depressed by these dreams, but then a friend pointed out what I was quite failing to see, that if what I was seeking was a new solution for myself, then it could not yet have a name. So, once more remembering Freud, I decided just to see what came now. What did come was the word "water." Unsure what to make of this I set out to see what use J had made of images of water, hoping it might clarify my own journeyings.

First, in the story book there are all the bridge pictures, bringing the water, which is, as both of us now agree, the wide flowing water of the river Thames. It is once described as something that could be fallen into and then climbed out of, but it is mostly shown as a carrier for boats. There had also been, on another level, his early fascination with what he had called J's "water hole" at just the time when he was learning control of his bladder; as well as the bit in the diary about his angrily "making water" on the floor when I had refused to hold his potty for him.

In addition, there was also the water of tears to be considered. As I have said, he did not cry very much, at least when I was there to hear it. The three times I remembered especially were the day he found the door shut when I was working, the morning when he had earache, and the day I told him about the breakdown of our marriage, but none of these were floods of tears.

When first surrounded by water

Nevertheless he did have some daydreams of flooding, for I now remembered that day when I was bathing him and he said "wouldn't it be a joke" if he hit one of the pipes, broke it and caused a "flooding!" I wondered, does the idea of it as a joke cover fear of wishing to drown me? But then he would be drowned too? Or might it perhaps also hint at a memory of when he really was all surrounded by water, before the "breaking of the waters" and in the place where all his needs were fulfilled? If so perhaps calling it a joke was not only defensive, but part of a wish to explore, in play, his own earliest experiences. Perhaps even the so big feet, in the pre-story book drawing of a little man, with its clearly marked navel, could be relevant here: even indicate a left-over trace of the time when his strongest spontaneous body movement was to wriggle and kick in the waters of my womb. He would then have experienced his feet as coming up against something that limited his activity, held it. Perhaps finding his very first experience of boundaries? Could it even be that he would have been pleased, when he made the big feet drawing, if I had told him how, when we had got off the Channel boat to land in France on our last holiday before he was born, he had kicked energetically; and I, delighted at being in France again, had then wondered if he had somehow been affected by this, so that the energetic wriggling and kicking could even have been his taking part in my delight? Or was the idea of drowning me more important? Or why not all of these?

But what about my own ideas on flooding? Most unexpectedly I heard some lines of verse running in my head:

O, down in the meadows the other day
A gathering flowers both fine and gay,
A gathering flowers both red and blue,
I little thought what love could do.

I recognised it as the bit of a folk song that I had used as the heading of the chapter called "What the eye likes" in my 1950 book about my own blocks over painting. And then another verse began to haunt me – John Donne's

O, more than Moone,
Draw not up seas to drown me in my sphere
Weep me not dead in thine arms. But forbeare
To teach the sea, what it may doe too soone.

I had originally put it at the top of a chapter supposed to be about fears in the use of colour and I had chosen it purely on impulse; how little I knew then what it might mean to me in the future, after so many years and through studying J's story book.

As for the gathering of flowers, I saw it now as a way of talking about what I had done in my first book, or rather in the diary that led up to it, which was, as I have said, trying to keep a record of what had seemed to be the most important thing that had happened the day before. I had then decided that making a note of happinesses did matter and should be attended to, if one was searching for a life of one's own. But what about its opposite? What about woes? I think I was then not ready to study those, even though the second quotation does give a hint of what was to come.

The caravan containers go deep into the earth

Instead of water, this so fluid thing from which, they say, all life started, now came its opposite, things with stable barriers, such as houses, boats – and caravans.

Recently I had been asking myself why J had done two drawings of the caravan. The first had a strange shape rising up from one end, which I had assumed was an attempt to indicate the shafts that the caravan would need if it were to be moved; I even thought I could see a hint of a horse's (front view) framed between the shafts. In the second picture these shafts are not there; however what struck me again about these two pictures was the so carefully drawn strong hooks from which hang two shapes that look like wooden buckets. I knew I had already seen these hanging shapes as some sort of containers, and when J (now 62) happened to turn up just after I had written this, he said (although he had before told me he had no memory at all of writing the book) that he felt sure they were buckets for water. What especially interested me was that these buckets hanging from those so strong hooks are shown, in both pictures, with their bases right below the level of the ground that supports the caravan wheels. Since he had also repeated this way of placing them in the second caravan picture, it did look as if it had a special meaning for him. Could it be that he already knew about the source of life, the water of life, which lies, for each of us, deep down below our common-sense everyday awareness? But on another level I suspect it must be something to do with his particular experience of having been weaned; as well as being related to two of his statements, noted in the diary – his own remarks that he is not going to "get dead," and that he will die when I do.

Feeling the weight of my arms

Whatever he meant by this placing of the buckets and their so strong hooks, it was my caravan that he was drawing, so it was even more clear that I must try to see how those hooks could apply to me. On my way to seeking an answer, I found myself thinking of J's picture in the story of the lighthouse keeper who puts new wicks and oil in the lamps – in fact, feeding them; and how in that picture the lighthouse keeper does have arms, unlike all the other little men, except for the one in the porter story.

Now, after writing this, suddenly something surprising happened. While I was writing this book, I had been regularly having what she called "play times" with a Matthias Alexander teacher (I call her K). She was rather a special one, using her own discoveries as well as his, and she had suggested the importance of walking while letting my arms hang freely, swinging, allowing the full flow of the experience of their weight. And when I did this, my whole idea of myself changed; I felt myself to be a quite different person, markedly transformed. It felt almost as if what had happened was that my hidden stone-throwing bit, and my usually so well-behaved everyday self had somehow come together, interpenetrated. And what was so important in all this was that as I walked across the room with my arms swinging freely, K had played at being frightened; she had shrunk away from me, actually laughing. What I had felt was a quiet kind of power that could, if necessary, be aggressive, a quite new feeling for me; and with it came the memory of J's delighted response to my game of walloping him when he was too slow going to bed.

So I queried, could it really be partly because of me that most of the little men have no arms? After all, one needs arms for stone-throwing as well as for hugging and holding. Was he becoming more able to draw men with arms because he intuitively knew that I would have to get nearer to accepting my stone-throwing self, without which he could not really accept his own?

No arms, no hands, no sex?

Thinking of armlessness, and therefore of no hands, of course led to the idea of anxiety over masturbating, even though the diary notes that J had cheerfully told his father how his "Albert" liked to be rubbed, and he had never been told not to do it. It therefore looks as if he had, when writing his stories, managed to split off ideas about such enjoyable manual activity from the daydreams of attacks on his father that he had once, even triumphantly, told me about and that I had noted in the diary.

As for my own childhood experiences, in the early 1900s anything to do with physical sex was totally barred from being spoken about. Although I had no memories of it, I was fairly certain that I would have been smacked by a nanny for any activity seen to be remotely masturbatory.

To go back to J's armless little men, there was of course the fact that his father, being unable to hold paid employment because of his illness, could easily be portrayed as armless; although, when he was well, Dennis was likely to be busy making something in his workshop and was always most helpful to J over the management of tools etc. Hence the lighthouse keeper with arms carrying the oil for the lanterns, as well as the one coming down to join in the game of dominoes, could both represent the hope of a fully restored father, complete with arms and so able to work, which would also mean that I could stay at home and have the brother or sister that his wolf wanted.

Speed of moving and the imaginative body

There was also J's emphasis on the slowness of the cara-van. Whatever it meant to him (my own slowness in understanding his story?) it did mean something special for me since, over very many years, I had been aware that I was always moving too quickly, in any practical activities (except when gardening). Connected with this was something I had previously called my "imaginative body" which seemed almost like a seamless all-enveloping inner garment which, when I moved at my own speed, felt as if it exactly coincided with the shape of my actual skin. But if I moved my hands and arms too quickly, as I nearly always did when doing chores in a hurry to get the job done, it felt as if something like an inner tearing had gone on, a tearing that could only be mended by stopping the activity, whatever it was, and letting my attention flood through the whole of my body, even into the ground while lying flat on the floor.

A physiotherapist I had once seen, because of backache, had said, "But you are so greedy." I had replied "Of course," knowing exactly what she meant. Moving too quickly felt like wanting to get too much done, and not only the amount but the way one did it, somehow jumping ahead of oneself. Again, I remembered J's little armless men and how it was shortly before he made his story book that Dennis and I had first become interested in Matthias Alexander's work, with its basic instruction about moving with "no end gaining." I hoped I had never held J with the get-it-done-quickly kind of attention in his babyhood, just as I never did while working in the garden – or had I?

Now came a very strange thought: "moving with no end gaining," could this even possibly be what the Christian gospel (Matthew 6:34) calls "taking no thought for the morrow"?

It was not until I was 13 that I had first become consciously aware that my mother always moved too quickly. Always taking thought for the morrow? It was in 1913, when we were all on holiday in Scotland and had set out to climb the mountain Cairngorm, and my brother had tried to help her up the steepest bits by pushing on her back, but she went so fast that he could not keep up with her.

This memory now took me right back to my own beginnings. I suspected that after she had fed me, she would have had the nanny put me straight back into the cot, no time being allowed for playing with her breast after feeding from it.

So, might it not be that learning how to move at one's own speed, with one's own inbuilt rhythms, could be a major aspect of learning how to be one's self, harder if you are the youngest, and always being told to hurry up or you will be left behind.

The snake-skin and seeing from behind one's eyes

Soon I came back again to the bodily meaning of the word "cross," that is, the horizontal line of my shoulders against my spine. I found myself wriggling them to release the backache that came just at the midpoint where the shoulder-line crosses the spine. As I did so a totally unforeseen phrase appeared, "shuffle off this mortal coil," and with it the memory of the so small snake-skin that I once brought back from Greece and wrote about:

I found it in the grass amongst the ruins in the island of Delos (birth place of Apollo, they said, so no one else was allowed to be born there). But had the owner of this small skin got itself born there? And was it here that it shuffled out of its old skin when it got too tight. It had shed even the skin of its eyes, here they are, tiny panes of clear skin. This weightless discarded relic that I hold in my hand, all latticed like a dragonfly's wing and with a dark zigzag down its back. Of course, it's an adder, I hadn't thought of that, an adder's bite can be dangerous, surely.

That's how I wrote about it more than thirty years ago, as one of my beads of memory. For me the fact of it having shed the skin of its eyes meant, and still does, seeing the world from behind my eyes instead of just with them. How differently I see the world when I do that and how differently I see myself; it feels as if I have sloughed off a skin, perhaps even several, a transformation of feeling. How very odd, it's such a simple inner gesture to see from behind one's eyes instead of just with them. Or is it? It means facing all the dark innerness, which is partly done by widening one's attention, as I once discovered, and later found it could also happen by just attending to one's breathing, how the world then immediately becomes paintable. And now it's the same sort of thing that happens, even if I do deliberately only a small bodily exercise, I suddenly notice that the pictures on the wall have sprung into new life.

Also the mere thought of my snake-skin now brings this change, both in my image of myself and the quality of what I am looking at; it brings a kind of doubleness of space, the dark inner one held simultaneously with the lighted outer one of the surrounding world, an interpenetration which is, I suppose, what a good drawing is a record of.

The unseen presence in the fig tree

But of course Hamlet, in taking off this mortal coil, is thinking about death, which I am too, since I am now 93. And what will happen to me then? I just don't know. Will there be some mysterious change? After all, I did make that picture, in Delphi, that called itself "And she, supposing him to be the gardener." Perhaps it will be like the startling change in what I was perceiving that I found when writing the book in Spain, when my images led me to that mentally wiping-myself-out gesture, that silent incantation "I know nothing, have nothing, want nothing"? I just don't even know what this "I" is that says it doesn't know. I just don't know what it really is, this something in J (see the diary) that could enable him to say "I am dancing" or that could make him hide himself and make me ask "Where is little J?" and then emerge, squealing with delight, saying "HERE he is!" Just what is this!?

Now comes a memory of myself wandering alone from the crowd on the hilltop which is said to be the ruins of Troy, and how I wrote:

I had picked all the wild flowers that I could find that were unknown to me. And then carrying this prickly bunch of nameless miracles I had come upon a great lusty fig tree, not dried up at all but flourishing among the rubble, its roots surely going down to secret sources of water and its leaves reaching to the air like a great free dome. I had glimpsed ripe figs and burrowing in to reach them had heard a rustle of leaves coming from the other side and thought there must be someone else there too, although I could see nothing but leaves. I had gone on picking till my cupped hands were full, vaguely supposing that it was some Greek boy that had been my hidden companion. But afterwards the image remained, the unseen presence within the green dome of the fig tree.

But what about this unseen presence? Of course it could have been malign, but at that moment of writing about it

I seem to have been more concerned with a benign one, something that I found it all too easy to forget. Unbelievably, I now heard in my head the phrase "The intolerable compliment of the love of God." Who said that? I don't know. But I have been the receiver of so much goodness in my life, what difference does it make to call it the goodness of God? Or the goodness of people, starting with having been given this so utterly mysterious thing we call life, given it by my parents, together with all their love and care, as well as countless other people since, both living and dead, and including all the beauty of the world. Shall I give the source of all goodness a label and call it G.O.D.? Or denote it by the crowned empty circle of the Kabbalah? Or to quote once more, "The Tao of which we speak is not the real Tao"?

But of course this must leave room for what I can learn from whatever J is trying to say when he puts the boats on his river, those outlined entities that are also containers and, unlike houses, are able to move. So may it not be that he is using them in order to say something about his awareness of people? Thus the boat with the dominoes game and the lighthouse keeper coming down to join in could be not only his hope for a happy family situation, but also, as part of this, hope for a not-anxious mother-me? Isn't this perhaps hinted at by the column of smoke going straight up from the big steamers in both the river pictures, indicating a calm windless day – i.e. a kind of serenity that I had myself by no means yet worked through to on a solid basis of accepting my own opposites of feeling? So what was central for what I could myself do? Was it really allowing the full flow of awareness down my arms, just by attending to it, the full awareness of their weight, the pull downwards as if deep into the earth, which is also the acceptance of my capacity to throw my weight about, the capacity to hurt with my arms "stone-throwing" as well as the capacity to embrace, both to create new shapes and also to be the taker of care. Could it be that it was this acceptance that would eventually free my hunched-up shoulders?

PART FIVE

Using my own pictures

6

Always protecting your mother

Turning words upside down

Then I had to face the fact that something very peculiar had been happening to me over the months of writing these chapters. It was that when reading a book or a newspaper or scientific article I would be apt, now and then, to read a single word as the opposite of what was printed; i.e. if the sentence contained a word such as "likely" I would read it as "unlikely," a trick that was obviously liable to make a total mess of the meaning of what I was trying to read. After a time I thought this must really be looked into; I had to ask just what was going on.

Always protecting your mother

Some ideas pointing in the direction of possible answers came when I remembered how, in recent years, an osteopath from whom I was seeking help for shoulder-cross backache had responded to my rather random talk by saying "Do you realise you are always protecting your mother?" At first I thought I knew all about this, since I had always, as I have said, remembered having been upset by my father's irritability with my mother after his breakdown. I thought my being so upset was because I felt she did not deserve it; I always thought of her as a loving and devoted person.

What my mother made me pray for

Clearly now I had to search my mind to find what else I might be continually trying to protect her from.

The first idea that came was that, when I was about 6, she had made me add to my nightly prayers, "Keep the door of my lips that I offend not with my tongue." This did suggest that up until then I had been quite capable of using my tongue in ways that could hurt, though I doubt whether it was against her, but rather against my five-years-older sister, who used to snub me fiercely, though I have only one conscious memory of a moment of great anger with her. But what was puzzling was that the prayer was apparently still having effect, for after all these years I still had great difficulty about expressing anger, combined with anxiety about having given offence by my tongue, even on occasions when it might have been right to do so.

The Mrs Punch drawing

Although I could not remember any occasion when I expressed my anger with my mother verbally, I did now remember a doodle drawing I made in great anger and published in my book about blocks over painting.[1]

It must have been made about a year or so before J made his story book and when I was already in intermittent Freudian psychoanalysis. I would certainly have shown it to my analyst but am fairly sure she said nothing about it. Also I do remember feeling that the anger which prompted the drawing was not with my mother, but with my mother-in-law over one or other of my husband's many infidelities. It had called itself both "Mrs Punch" and "The Duchess" (from *Alice in Wonderland*)[2] who I thought was always saying "Off with her head!" (Or was it the Red Queen who said that?)

Surprised that I had to return to this drawing after more than fifty years, I next had to consider just what sort of opposites it portrays. At once I found myself asking, "Isn't she the opposite of all I like to think of myself as being, just as the stone-throwing woman in J's story was? And do I feel she is so repulsive just because she has been totally cut off

[1] Marion Milner, *On Not Being Able to Paint* [1950], Hove: Routledge, 2010.
[2] Ibid., p. 5.

Mrs Punch

from the bit of me that I find acceptable?" Could she even be a bit of myself that got locked away after that prayer my mother insisted on? Have the implications of this only come to awareness since the day I walked with free-swinging arms, feeling their full weight? Could it even be that this could only happen because my Alexander teacher had been able to play at cowering away from me in mock terror, and actually laughed, thus showing she was not afraid of my "Off with her head" self and could survive it? Is this even the reason why the picture calls itself "Mrs Punch," as well as being the beheading Red Queen (slightly disguised by calling her The Duchess)? Also, the magazine *Punch* was all out to make people laugh. But also "all that swank of jewellery" said my original thought about it, and surely that could sound like envy?

Swinging arms and couch analysis

However, my mother, though very pretty, was a most modest person, no swank about her at all, but no Mrs Punch element either, not able to laugh at herself as my father could. Thus I had never for a moment consciously thought of my Mrs Punch–Red Queen drawing as a picture of her, nor, at the time of making it, had I thought of it as a picture of a bit of me, perhaps of me secretly mocking the woman who had been my analyst when I made the picture? In fact was it possible that I had never come to guess it could be a part of myself, just because in all my "couch" analyses it had never even occurred to me to get up and walk about with my arms swinging freely? And would any of my analysts have been able to laugh and play at being frightened if I had? Of course not, quite against the rules. And yet it seemed that it was just this bodily action that had made it possible for me to realise that this horrible Mrs Punch was a hidden part of me, since I could feel in my swinging arms a certain capacity for arrogant ruthlessness, but which could also seem funny in its assumption of queenly absolute power. Thus I now had to face the fact that in some split-off part of myself I could be saying "off with her head"; in fact, a bit of matricide based on rivalry?

And to think that it could only be by means of my free-swinging arms being noticed and reacted to with laughter that this commonplace of Freudian theory had at last come home to me!

In short, could this be really what I felt I had to protect my mother from, so much more than just from my father's actual irritability? However, the Mrs Punch figure looks partly male, so is she not also a mother who contains within her the authority of one's father, and thus, behind that, the authority of the Law and the State? This reminded me that the nearest I could get to ideas of anger with my mother was when, sometimes, as a child, if told by her to do something I did not want to do, I would say, "Why should I?" and she would answer, "Because I say so."

As for the theme of rivalry with her, I now remembered that I had in my possession a little drawing that I painted eighty years ago, and put at the beginning of the illustrated Nature Diary which I had begun to keep at the age of 11, and continued for nearly ten years, because I wanted to be a naturalist and had read that naturalists keep notes. The first entry, with picture, is dated 1911 and says, "Saw a drake and two wild ducks." But the picture shows only one duck, so I thought now that it looks as if I felt that one of us had to go.

My way out of this impasse seems to have been to shift my interest to the study of Mother Nature, a subject which was, as I have said, my father's interest, not my mother's, and also something which would be able to survive all attacks by me (at least in 1911).

The two beech trees

Close to the Mrs Punch picture was another of my drawings in my 1950 painting book.[3]

One that did now suggest to me a great anger with both my parents, as separate beings. I had made it at the beginning of the Hitler war when, as an evacuee family, we were living in the borrowed cottage in Sussex. (It must have been about six months after J had made his story book which, unknown to us, was then remaining, unfound, in our London house.)

So, at leisure here in Sussex, because my work had had to stop with the outbreak of the war, I had one day sat down to draw two huge splendid beech trees that I had delighted in. What appeared on my paper were two little stunted bushes struggling against a raging blizzard. At the time when I first wrote about the drawing, I had seen the theme of opposites but not risked exploring more fully the implications of this. Now, however, I could ask more bravely just what my unconscious was up to in turning those so magnificent trees into scrubby little bushes.

Undoubtedly at the time of making the drawing I had felt the two trees to be immensely powerful presences, so it was not easy to see them as standing for idealised images of my parents, images that I had in the hinterland of my mind turned into their exact opposite, not stately at all but so small that they are in danger of being uprooted by the blizzard. But why? Was my unknown self here playing the opposites game just for the fun of it? Or did it mean that in some remote part of myself I did feel I had achieved such an imaginative castration of parental power? If so, might it not account for my sometimes recurrent moods of feeling helpless impotence, an inability to get even ordinary jobs

[3] Ibid., pp. 7–8.

Heath fire

Two beech trees

done, chores etc., much less any truly creative activity? In these moods, could my internal parent images (unknown to me because of my angry wishes being denied) be here felt reduced to such a helpless struggle against being uprooted by the blizzard?

Unbearable dependence?

Even if such a secret cold blizzard of scorn of authority did exist in me, I felt it could be there to cover up something even more disturbing, an early totally felt terror about the precariousness of one's own existence. Could this drawing possibly be an example of trying imaginatively to make impotent the parental powers just because of being unable to bear knowing one's total dependence on them? Might it not be hiding such an amount of terror, especially if one had had to emerge too soon from an illusion that one had oneself created the world just by opening one's eyes – or even one's bowels?

Only one person in the world?

I wondered now, might J not also have been expressing a momentarily glimpsed memory of such an infant illusion when he asked Joyce, "Is there more than one person in the world?" Not only this, but there was also an opposite view, i.e. his comment, after I had read to him out of the Book of Genesis the passage where God says "Let there be light" and J had said, "You know, I think it was like that."

So also there was his insistence, again perhaps only momentarily believed, that he would die when I did. Was I perhaps right to see this as a memory of a time when he was necessarily not yet fully accepting the gap, the separateness, between him and me, and therefore between him and the world?

Here too I could not help remembering how, quite a number of years after making the J diary and during the war, a patient of mine who in fact managed to get herself to me day by day, was yet able to say she was utterly terrified of the bombing, just because she felt that she herself was everything, so the bomb was bound to fall on her.

One's lovely stuff

Following on the idea of feeling as if one had created the world oneself, my memories now took another leap forward to a time about ten years after J had made his story book. It was a memory of another boy, this one aged 11, who was coming to me for child psychoanalysis, partly because of a bout of backwardness at school, but who was deeply interested in a chemistry set he had at home. One day, in our analytic session, he had said to me, "What is your name?" and I had to say the name of a certain chemical, to which he answered, "It's lovely stuff, I have made it." I had been glad to be, for a time, the lovely stuff that he had made, and grateful for the hint he had given me to do with stages in coming to recognise the otherness of the so-called external world.

One's parents' creativity

If this was at all near the truth of the blasted beech tree pictures, then what of my feeling about my parents' actual creation of me, and of my sister and brother before me? I had only one memory on the subject of curiosity about baby-making, and it was a memory of being firmly snubbed. I was about 9 or 10, and all I thought I knew on the subject was having heard it said that people got fat when they were going to have a baby. So when our mother's help, known as Simp, said to my mother, "You are getting fatter," I had said, "Hooray, p'raps she is going to have a baby!" But Simp had said "NEVER say anything like that again!" I was so terribly compliant, it seems, that I did not even dare to think any more about such matters. I even remember how, a little later, being taken by my mother on a social visit to a woman who must have been very pregnant, what I had said to myself was "No wonder they always tell one to stand up straight, if that is what happens to you tummy if you don't!"

On the other hand, as recorded in the diary, J had shown open curiosity and interest about the whole process of baby-making. However there are also hints of complicated and anxious ideas about it; for instance his daydream of a man lying on a railway close to a farm, who would not be hurt when a train came because he had armour on.

Dancing trees

Still thinking about the drawing of the two beeches now brought to my mind the cover of J's book. Here he also has put two trees. Out of the corner of my eye I now suddenly saw them as dancing beside each other. Weren't there dancing trees somewhere in the diary, where a rabbit and a squirrel came together to make babies?

7

Two new free drawings

I now thought, why not try again drawing freely and see what happens? I wondered whether what came would be like those kinds of miscellaneous figures that had appeared in 1938, some of which I had put in the painting book. This time I decided to draw with my left hand (I am actually right-handed), partly because in J's under-the-porter-story little man drawing it is his left hand that is shown as dark, so I thought it was my left hand that would be most likely to have access to ideas of the darkly hidden powers.

I drew in charcoal with my eyes open but in a dreamy way, not thinking what might be appearing, and after several totally confused scribbles with nothing to be said about them, there had appeared what seemed to me to be a head, with an open jaw and a single tooth. It called itself "Alligator." Immediately I found myself back at my J diary and before that at the pain I had felt at his one and only moment of biting me. Did this really mean that I must face the possibility that this drawing, of what to me looked like an open jaw, could be a picture of my own alligator bit, hungrily sucking and apparently very early split off, so that it had survived in the deep archaeological layers of my psyche, and was somehow now seeking recognition through my drawing? But why so long buried?

A possible answer came from a surprising moment that occurred about the time when the drawing appeared; I had suddenly felt a pang in my heart at the sight of the empty plate from which I had just eaten a satisfying meal. This raised many questions. First, was this the destruction that J seemed to be battling with when he dictated the picture letter to be sent to me with its idea of a devouring dragon? Also did he so need an answer from me in order to be sure I had not been devoured by his terrible dragon self? Secondly, knowing as I did that this was an example of the everyday stuff of psychoanalytic theory, why was it that I could still be experiencing such a sudden pang? I knew, because my mother had told me, about her having to wean me suddenly at 4 months because she had a breast abscess. Thus it would seem that there had been little chance of me slowly learning that my devouring intentions had not been an actuality? So, was there really, still hidden away in my secret inner world, a belief that I had had the power to destroy, with the "door of my lips" and of my jaws, just what I most needed and valued?

Contemplating the jaws drawing now reminded me that, not long before beginning this study of the J diary and story book, I had developed a bad pain in my upper and lower jaws and my doctor had diagnosed angina, though adding that it was unusual to feel the pain first in the jaw. Sometimes I would even be woken at night by the pain, so it could not be due just to strain on the heart muscle as a result of excess physical exertion. This reminded me too that my mother had also told me (long after my couch analyses were over) that, before weaning me, she had had to wear a nipple shield because of the pain from my sucking.

Further, if it is true, as they say it is, that most babies gaze into their mother's eyes while sucking at her breast, could it then be that I had seen in her eyes the pain I was causing? But was not yet separated out enough for it to be known as a "not-me" pain? Could it be that it was coming back now as pain in my own jaws? Once more, as I had before in the painting book, I wondered, could it even be that this is what William Blake was talking about with his lines:

The caterpillar on the leaf
Repeats to thee thy mother's grief

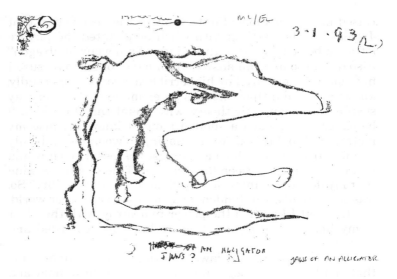

Jaws of an alligator

— lines that he puts in two places, and that made G. K. Chesterton say in his book on Blake that they are so utterly meaningless they would prove the poet's madness?

A creature in agony

In order to try to understand more of this I had done another left-hand drawing and this one did not just remind me of physical pain, I even had a pang of angina when trying to describe what the picture said to me. I had written down my first thoughts about it:

> I see it as a creature in agonising pain, its open mouth suggesting a smothered cry, almost as if it feels it has no hope of the cry being understood and help arriving. I almost feel it is caught in a flash moment of realising that it can be its own loving that causes pain to the other. If so the spikes on its back suggest it feels it can't be hugged and comforted, it has even to warn that its

loving is dangerous. And it is top-heavy, with only very shadowy feet, no certain hold on the outer supporting world. Almost like a child in a night terror who can't accept the reality of the loving arms that are trying to give comfort, it is too immersed in an inner world of past catastrophic happenings, even the loved image of the comfort-giver felt to be either destroyed or turned revengeful.

Having contemplated this agonised creature I now found another diary note that I had just written, intended for my own use, but now it seemed relevant here:

I don't seem able to look at people's eyes, to know what they are feeling, the shape of their mouths seems to tell me so much more (except when they wear beards). Maybe I don't dare look? For fear of seeing the pain that was in my mother's eyes? Or is it that to see is also to be seen? Do I dread they will see the so denied alligator bit of me?

Could this possibly be why the prayer she made me say had worked inhibitingly for so long? Could it even have been taken by me to mean that my loving with my mouth was to hurt, which is much more of a disaster than to think of one's hate or anger as hurting, since that is most often what they are meant to do, meant to force the other to do what one wants – or even intended to hurt in order to get one's own back for some hurt to oneself.

And what about the shadowiness of the creature's feet? Certainly, if it was me, they are only metaphorically like that; throughout my life I have had unfailing enjoyment from my actual feet, I even won a medal for ballroom dancing and once achieved dancing on skates. But metaphorically true, yes, because I have always known I was hooked on a difficulty over openly expressing disagreement with people, i.e. standing on my own feet; often not even allowing myself to know that I did not agree, even a compulsion to be in agreement with anyone I was close to.

Having known about this for years, and knowing that my couch analysis had not altered it, I had originally

A creature in agony

linked it with my father's inability to stand any kind of quarrelling. However, in recent years it had occurred to me that my mother had, almost certainly not even admitting it to herself, a sense of depression about herself and also deep disappointment over her marriage. So had I always been unwittingly protecting her, not just from my offending, hurting with my lips, but also by agreeing implicitly with her own ways of being oblivious to her own sorrows?

One's own feet on the ground?

Following on my surprise at finding this agonised creature produced by my left hand, I now found I had a need to do some more of the free association kind of writing, and to do more on the word "feet." I found I had written:

Why are its feet so shadowy in the drawing? No firm feeling of being on the ground of Mother Earth? "From whom we live and move and have our being"? Wrong surely, the Bible says "IN WHOM we live and move and have our being." But FROM WHOM is right too, "from whom" comes all the food through which we do "live and move" etc. Yes, but "in whom" is right too, the whole of human culture within which, or special bits of it, we do exist and have our being. Perhaps this is what J was dimly feeling after, when he spoke of "the people" in the dominoes bridge picture?

Continuing my speculations about the drawing of the too shadowy feet, I was brought back to the word gravity and my discovery of the quite new sense of my self that had come from the feeling of the weight of my free-swinging arms while walking. So now I had to speculate whether there might not be a connection between this and J's putting those so strong hooks on the hanging containers in his drawing of my caravan. Also their bases going down below the surface of the ground suggesting even an awareness of the pull towards the very core of Mother Earth. If so, could my drawing of the so shadowy feet then be partly about my not yet having entirely found my own feet, to do with what I believed about my relation to whatever is the ultimate reality of the universe, including all the agonies of suffering that are experienced in this particular planet's bit of it, as well as the unbelievable beauties and joys?

Mending the hurts

More and more I now thought that when I held J in my arms all day, after his earache, without either of us having to use the doors of our lips, it was vitally important for both of us. Also that my capacity to keep the silence had come slowly, out of a growing ability to digest all that I had been driven to write about, both at the beginning of his life (1932) after the six a.m. feed, and also during my time in Spain.

J's feet and a new sense of trust

It was here that I found myself having to think more about why J might have had to put the chalice shape in one of the chimney-pots' space. I had the idea that he could have been trying to find form for a kind of feeling that, however much in the past he had felt that there had been a dead mother, in his inner world I was now resurrected. It could be that he felt that during the seven years of his life, much inner and outer work had been done, enough to make possible a trust in a restored source of goodness in himself. And surely this must be based on memories of being fed and cared for as an inner and outer work had been done, enough to make possible a trust in a restored source of goodness in himself. And surely this must be based on memories of being fed and cared for as an infant and throughout childhood, including all that schooling had done for him, enough to enable him, at last, to have his own feet, not just when sitting still as in the second caravan picture, but also the feet – although only tiny – are now actually pointing away from the station towards the bridge and the railway line. But also, what about the fact that he had used a religious symbol? Didn't this link with his having liked making what he had called cathedrals in his earlier years – that is sacred spaces, holy spaces – to do with wholeness, just as pictures (good ones) are?

8

Play of making collages from my old failed paintings

Making collages

Not only was I discovering, through meditating on the diary and story book, something that had apparently not been adequately realised in my own couch analysis, there was another activity of my own which was now calling attention to itself, one which I first looked on as just playing. It was that during the last ten or so years working with patients I had been enjoying tearing or cutting up what I considered to have been my own failed paintings and then picking out the bits of colour or shapes that I particularly liked, putting them in a heap on a tray, and letting my wandering eye, often only out of its corner, select any of them that caught my attention. I would then arrange these on a sheet of paper, just shifting them around until some sort of intriguing pattern emerged, which I would then paste up to make a collage. Eventually each of these would tell me what it was about. There was only one rule I set myself, that they should not be abstract pictures, they should rather represent some sort of human (or animal) encounter, although the background could be abstract. Since often quite subtle colour was the basic element in them, they are not suitable for reproducing here, but there are some which can be shown in black and white.

There was one which called itself "The Temperamental Hen" (see colour plate section). I saw that on the right is a hen, she looks very excited and is surely offending with her tongue. On the left is a very narrow upright figure: it seemed that it could be seen as an apt image of the kind of God I felt I had been made to pray to, as a child, to get my tongue controlled in a way that my mother approved of. As such, it seemed a bit like the one I had heard of in the Athanasian Creed. A God who seemed to be saying that anyone who does not believe in Jesus cannot be saved (whatever that means), so I had worried about all the millions of people who had never had a chance to hear of Jesus. The narrow figure in the picture is saying "You can't talk to me like that!"

There was another collage that called itself "The Listeners" (see colour plate section) that especially surprised me, both by its content and the way it had happened. It had arrived through my having cut out from an old painting of mine what looked vaguely like two figures standing side by side, the cutting out of course leaving a two-figure-shaped hole in the original failed painting. Looking at these shapes, I had suddenly felt like putting a patch of black paper behind the two holes and then I cut this black bit into the shape of the holes. Thus I now had two figures side by side which I had then placed in the centre of an unspecified background. The resulting collage at first made me think of Walter de la Mare's poem "The Listeners" which I had always loved, but never felt I had understood, so this is what I called the picture.

The Listeners*

Is there anybody there? Said the Traveller,
Knocking on the moonlit door
And his horse in the silence champed the grasses
Of the forest's ferny floor:
And a bird flew up out of the turret,
Above the Traveller's head.
And he smote upon the door again a second time;
"Is there anybody there?" he said.
But no one descended to the Traveller:

* With kind permission from The Literary Trustees of Walter de la Mare and The Society of Authors as their representative.

No head from the leaf-fringed sill
Leaned over and looked into his grey eyes
Where he stood perplexed and still.
But only a host of phantom listeners
That dwelt in the lone house then
Stood listening in the quiet of the moonlight
To that voice from the world of men;
Stood thronging the faint moonbeams on the dark stair
That goes down to the empty hall
Hearkening in an air stirred and shaken
By the lonely Traveller's call.
And he felt in his heart their strangeness
Their stillness answering his cry,
While his horse moved, cropping the turf,
'Neath the starred and leafy sky;
For he suddenly smote on the door, even
louder, and lifted his head:
"Tell them I came, and no one answered,
That I kept my word," he said.
Never the least stir made the listeners,
Though every word he spake
Fell echoing through the shadowiness of the still house
From the one man left awake:
Ay, they heard his foot upon the stirrup,
And the sound of iron on stone,
And how the silence surged softly backward,
When the plunging hoofs were gone.

Next I had to ask myself, not what is this poem really
saying, which I don't know, but what is the poem saying to
me? First it is certainly about a house, but it has no cats or
people at the windows, as one of J's houses had. And just
who is the lone traveller, who has a capital T in the first half
of the poem, but only a small h for "he" in the rest? Certainly
he is very bodily, he has a heart to feel with, he knocks, he has
grey eyes, he speaks, he has a horse that he mounts, and feet
that he puts noisily into the stirrups – all in contrast with the
silence and stillness of the house. And it seems his coming is
fulfilling a promise. But what about these listeners? Instead
of anybody being there as the traveller asks, instead of a

somebody, a self, there is a throng of phantoms, though these
do seem to have enough body to crowd together on the stairs.
I do feel that they are almost like a self that has had to get
disembodied and disperse itself, perhaps out of panic. Could
it then be a poem about madness, retreat from the world of
men, of whole human beings embodied here in the voice of
the Traveller? Also, there are stairs, as in J's see-through
house, and the phantoms seem to be staying at the top, they
don't come down to the empty hall. Thronged together at the
top, this makes me think of J's little cock-eyed house on the
hillside, with its too big window under the roof. So could
the phantoms then be disembodied thoughts that dare not
come down the stairs together and become a person who
could answer the knock on the door? Not like J, who wanted
one of his sun-babies to join up with him, and one to whom
he actually gave his own name.

But this change from the capital letter for the Traveller,
and the bit about fulfilling a promise – that could surely
relate to the Christian belief in the Second Coming of Christ,
but with something of disillusion about it, hinted at by the
sound of iron on stone as he goes away – "Iron, cold iron
shall be master of men all"?

Next, what happened was that, having left my Listeners
collage hanging on my studio wall, a visitor saw it and
suddenly said, "Of course, it's the Bible story of the walk to
Emmaus." Now, for the first time I could see that there was
an extra much larger shape on the right that could almost
be seen as a human figure – that of Jesus?

The Bible story

As I now remembered St Luke's account, it describes how
two of Jesus's disciples were walking towards a village
called Emmaus, near Jerusalem (I was told there is no such
place on any map), on the third day after the crucifixion.
A stranger appears and asks what they are talking about.
They say, "Oh, didn't you know, it's about Jesus of Nazareth,
who we thought would redeem Israel, and how he has been
crucified." According to St Luke, the stranger now walks
along with them, explaining at length how this was all

foretold in the Hebrew scriptures. When he was about to go
on his way, they asked him to stay and go with them to the
village. While having supper together, at the moment of his
breaking some bread, they suddenly recognise him as Jesus,
and he then disappears.

Being reminded of the passage from the Bible now
took me back to J's Station Hotel picture and this fact of
his having put a chalice shape on one of the chimney
tops, for this connected with a present-day intermittent
preoccupation of my own. It was that for some time I had
found myself pondering on the Christian gospels' accounts
of Jesus continually going off to pray alone in the desert,
and how, with death impending, he must have come upon,
or received, the idea of the ritual through which he wanted
to be remembered by his disciples, that is, the ceremonial
eating of bread and drinking of wine, these to be seen as his
body and his blood, and therefore a cannibalistic act.

The breaking of bread

According to the gospel accounts that I had been brought
up with, this ceremonial was to be the central way
of maintaining his disciples' relation to him after his
resurrection, and also to confirm their belief in what was
his central message about what he had called the Father.
As I had understood it, this was his word for what other
religions have named differently – Brahman, Jehovah,
Allah – all standing for whatever ultimate reality is, and
each having its different rituals. It seemed, from the gospel
accounts, that this ritual instituted by Jesus was in order
to embody his conviction that the ultimate reality is both
personal and totally loving, like a perfectly loving father;
even to the extent of total self-giving, as Jesus goes to a cruel
death on the cross, as a way of demonstrating the actuality
of that love. Also that this act of total self-surrender was
itself redeeming, a forgiving of all the sins of the world, in
so far as that love is accepted, also thereby guaranteeing
"eternal life." Apart from any theological aspects of these
gospel accounts, I now found myself having to face the fact
that this ritual that he had put as central for how he wanted

to be remembered, did embody a cannibalistic act. So I had to ask myself, had it taken these near two thousand years for another man (for did not Jesus always insist on calling himself "son of man"), for another man, Freud, as a result of listening to his patients and his own dreams, to notice and make basic to his own ideas about what being human really means, notice the fact that we are all cannibalistic in our infant loving desires, i.e. we are all unable to accept that what we love is not entirely our own.

Two friends talking

To go back again to my Listeners picture, I now noticed that there are little sparks of light around the heads of the two central figures, but could not at first think they made any particular kind of sense. However, since my visitor had seen the picture as representing the story of the walk to Emmaus, I did remember that the Bible account adds that the two men had said to each other, after Jesus had vanished, "Did not our hearts burn within us when we were walking with him and listening to him?" Quite apart from what we believe about the resurrection of Jesus, I had always liked this story, but was now astonished that my so unpremeditated collage, made just for fun, had somehow produced this halo effect on the two men walking together.

The green baby

Wondering some more about these two dark figures in the Listeners collage, I now found myself having to think more about the different things I had done when making them. Certainly they had emerged after I had made another collage, which called itself "The Green Baby trying to make sense of the world" (the baby being shown as a tiny green head at the bottom right corner; see colour plate section). In the large face in the middle, where the lips should be, there are two upright figures standing side by side with the dim shape of an infant between them. Here I remember again how when I originally cut out these two shapes from another old failed painting, seemingly in pure play, it had left a double-shaped hole, which I had then backed with a bit of black paper, the result being the two black figures of the Listeners picture, the one in which my visitor had seen the figure of Christ being recognised in the breaking of bread.

Still further wondering, I had to ask myself, could it be that the original figures I had cut out of the old painting and the double hole this had left, had implicitly come to stand for the feelings of emptiness when my parents were away together after my father's breakdown and all this just at the time when my school noticed my hunched left shoulder? Also could it even be that behind this feeling of loss there was also a more deeply hidden memory of the sudden loss of warm contact of my infant lips with my mother's breast? If so, what about those little sparks of light around the heads of those two dark figures in the "Listeners" picture? I had no idea whatever about how they could have got there, but, having got there, they did somehow suggest a hope that the two black emptinesses might eventually become filled by something new, since the two standing figures in the Green Baby picture's "mouth" do have the dim shape of an infant between them. Incidentally the "mouth" in the Green Baby picture does look almost as though it is saying "Hello," even shouting to someone across a wide space or long gap of time.

Once, some years before beginning this book, I found I had written a poem – or it had written itself (the first for more than forty years) – which actually called itself:

Mind the gap

("What is mind, no matter?
"What is matter, never mind".) Who said this?

"Mind the gap!" shouts the mechanical voice at the Embankment Tube station.
"Mind the gap!"
I do, I did, I never have fallen between the platform and the train
I don't mind, it doesn't matter.
Or does it?

I do mind the gap between what I can dream of and what
I can do.
And I do mind the gap between what I can dream of the
earth
And what we are doing to it.
Destroying the living matter on which we depend for life –
like the Amazon forests.

By now it seems that my problem of trying to heal my
body-mind split has, perhaps only temporarily, narrowed
itself down to noticing the moments when my hunched left
shoulder spontaneously lets itself down, and trying to hear
just what it may be saying by doing this. I notice it most often
when I am drinking and my lips are in contact with the edge
of the cup. When down, it seems to bring with it a sense of
quietness and safety. But all too soon it goes up again.

Woe-be-gone

There was yet another collage, amongst the twenty or so
which I had got framed and hung on my studio wall so that
they could talk to me or to any of my friends who might have
ideas about what they are saying. This was one that I myself
kept putting off listening to. It looks like a small solitary
phallic-shaped figure in front of two great rocks, and calling
itself "Woebegone," and that is what it looks like to me (see
colour plate section).

At first I wondered if it could be standing for an idea
of my father, banished miserably in my imagination into a
desert place because I could not bear his irritability with my
mother after his breakdown. But is there not also a kind of
pun on the word "Woebegone," since it can be split into woe-
be-gone, which is what I am beginning to guess I have been
trying to say for much of my life? And why? Could it be that
underneath the usual cheerfulness of my self-to-the-world
there has been a hidden woe, that my parents were not
happy, as well as a terrible fear of myself being abandoned
in a desert place, if I offended with my tongue?

But now the picture has something else to say, something which shows, again, how helpful friends can be in this

task of trying to communicate with one's unknown self. It happened when a woman friend (also a painter) had seen a copy of the picture and tried to draw my attention to what she saw as a golden face in profile, at the bottom right side of the picture. For several days I could not see it, but then, suddenly, I saw that the face in profile is looking calmly down beyond the edge of the frame, its expression full of peace. Also, that the top part of the head is covered by what looks like a golden helmet shape. So I began to see the head as trying to express a kind of trustfulness in what is hidden, trust in what one does not yet know; in fact, once more, trust in emptiness, trust in the gap in knowing. But then I saw that there is a dark line across the helmet, looking like a crack. One thought comes, is there here a reference to how cracked I was at Woking when I thought I was really a boy, thus blotting out the evidence of my own eyes, just as I had now quite failed to see the golden helmet part of the picture till the friend pointed it out?

Disillusion over what one has to give

But now I could see there was still another aspect of the picture; it is that the two great looming shapes that I had called rocks now look like buttocks with a dark passage between them that could be either a rectum or a vagina. This idea at first took me right back to J and his little friend proudly parading their full potties in the garden. So I wondered, is there another kind of woe, even of despair, not only of being helplessly stranded and abandoned, but also a feeling of hopelessness about what one has to give to the world, the disillusion of discovering that what felt like a loving gift from one's own body was totally rejected, thrown away, put down the drain. Here I thought, it's no wonder that there is such a high rate of suicide amongst the young unemployed, as they continue to find that nobody wants what they have to give.

This theme of early disillusion about what one has to give links up with early childhood problems in coming to distinguish the various bodily orifices. It reminded me of a little 11-year-old girl patient who would not speak to me at all for weeks, but sat at the table with her back to me, writing messages on lavatory paper and dropping them down her back for me to pick up off the floor. And how, eventually, I managed to say I thought that she was afraid that the air from her mouth would smell like the air from her bottom. At once she began to talk, and soon painted a lovely little water-colour picture of a girl dancing. In the end she said that psychoanalysis was the best thing that had ever happened to her.

Helmet

There was no doubt that for me the golden helmet covering the peaceful face brought back thought of what I wrote about in 1956, "the spontaneous inner force making for wholeness"; or, in different words, "the divinity that shapes our ends, rough hew them how we will." The helmet could then be put there to protect me from interferences with this spontaneous order, as well as against a woe which I feared could be unbearable. But then, did the crack in it mean it was a silly thing to hope for such a protection? But a crack can also be something through which light can penetrate in a pitch-dark place.

PART SIX

Different kinds of order

9

Words made flesh

By now, totally taken aback by my associations to what had
called itself "The Listeners" collage, and getting on for 96, I
am having doubts about whether I can get this book finished
before I am dead. I therefore decided to use the diary form
once more because it is quicker.

Woken by right hip pain (arthritis). Didn't Jacob have
hip trouble after wrestling with the angel all night? But
also woke to find myself saying "Three episodes from the
life of Christ." Surprised by this and before asking just
what these might be, I find myself writing "Am I now
feeling pain, not just writing about it or drawing images
of it? Am I now undoing my denials of it, negating the
negation, as Blake would say? Am I now feeling psychic
pain about how for much of my life I have often been so
dim-witted in my actions about people close to me?

Hasn't someone once said "Hold your bones gently?"
Instead of this busy purposiveness that I still get caught
up in. I have been told that one of the most holy icons in
Greece (I never saw it) is of Christ cradling his mother
on his lap instead of the other way round. But what
about that "three episodes" phrase that I woke up with?
First comes "Forgive them for they know not what they
do," said from the agony of hanging on the cross by
someone who insisted on calling himself "son of man."
Even if all the accounts of the life of this son of man are
not literally true in a historical sense, even if things
did not happen just like that, I feel the accounts can be

true in a far deeper than literal sense, which is surely why Blake was able to call out "Oh Human Imagination, Divine Body, I thee crucify"? So these words from the cross, what a staggering ideal for other sons (and daughters) of men, what a triumph of selfhood being let go. Also Blake is here bringing together words that are often thought of as opposites, "human" and "divine," "imagination" and "body." If that is the first episode of my three, what then is the second? The answer comes, "Touch me not for I am not yet ascended." And with this comes the memory of that collage I made twenty-five years ago in Delphi, that called itself "And she, supposing him to be the gardener." Only now can I have glimpses of its implications. Surely it tells of something new in the process of happening, everywhere, anywhere? And in me, negating the negations, especially of woe? Coming to know that woe, when accepted, does bring new life? I was just going to say, what is the third episode? I don't yet know. But yes, I do. It is "Blessed are they that mourn for they shall be comforted."

Isn't this expressing the same truth as "Except a grain of wheat fall into the ground and die it abideth alone ..." which surely means, how many psychic deaths one has to die in order to be able to grow? Which brings me to the question of what I want my own funeral to be like and so to the problem of my love-hate feelings about the Christian Church. Am I perhaps really a Christian even if a heretical one? I do love the Bible and if it wasn't for the Church we would never have had this so beautiful English translation of all that Middle Eastern expression of its own poetic genius. Certainly I am enthralled by those parables that Jesus told, they seem to me to give continual values about how to try to manage my life fruitfully – or what remains of it. In fact, I sometimes find myself thinking that they provide a sort of handbook for the processes of making anything new. For instance, all those gorgeous cathedrals could be both a product of and a celebration of that very thing, the act of creation. But I am also appalled by what terrible things have been done by the churches in the name of dogma about Jesus, such as the Crusades, the Inquisition, dogmas which in their literalism lend themselves to political exploitation, especially when joined up with nationalism.

What follows next is not diary writing, but my inventing for myself a particular mind-body incantation, in fact one in which I act out yet another experience of the meeting of opposites, that is, the spoken word and the silent bodily sensation. It is the act of simply naming a part of my body, while attending to the sensation of that bit of body's weight held by the floor. And this has had the effect of at once relieving its tension, and adding an increased sense of truly being. It had come about through an exercise of lying flat on my back on the floor and naming, first my heels then slowly working upwards, saying calves, buttocks, ribs (including elbows and hands, since my arms are lying outstretched by the side of me), shoulder blades, and ending with head, i.e. the back of it. On good days before I reach my head I feel fully relaxed and either ready to sleep or to get on with whatever needs to be done, according to circumstances. The point about each floor contact going with each word seems to be that it brings an awareness of losing any sense of skin boundary at that spot, a sense of being mixed up with what supports me, no distinct dividing line. And this seems to be an essential part of the relaxing process, since it also results in stilling all my inner chatter of imagined or remembered conversations with people, which so often go on in my head. But this also joins up with a sensation of the stilling of my lips, which feels like an acceptance of silence, a word that has echoes on so very many levels.

But there was also something else that I noticed: it was that when I do my new "words made flesh" exercise I quite often get stuck just before the level of feeling aware of the weight of my arms and shoulder blades, and I then either go to sleep or forget I am doing the exercise. But if I do go on and feel the weight of my outstretched arms and elbows, then a kind of inner stream or flow seems to come from each arm, which then meet at the base of my neck. And this meeting sometimes brings with it a feeling for which the phrase "living water" seems right. Oh, where does that phrase "living water" come from? Of course, it is the woman of Samaria who wanted not to have to come to the well everyday to fill her bucket, and thought Jesus was offering that kind of water. But what about the blocks which happen so often before I reach the level of my shoulder blades and outstretched arms? Is it because it is too close to ideas about the pain of crucifixion?

It was actually after more meditating on J's use of the form of the cross that I found myself continually being drawn back to my "Listeners" collage with its association to the de la Mare poem of that name; also to my friend's seeing in my picture the gospel story of the two disciples walking to the village of Emmaus, as well as the presence of a third (much taller) figure.

At the same time there was another thought hovering on the horizon of my awareness, and linked to J's use of the chalice form on the chimney-top space. It was a memory of the gospel account of Jesus going up into the desert places to pray I found myself wondering, at what stage did he decide that the central ritual by which he wanted to be remembered after his death would be a cannibalistic one – the eating of his body in the form of bread and drinking of his blood in the form of wine; a ritual which surely was metaphorically re-enacting one's very earliest impulses towards what one needed to maintain one's life, at one's mother's breast. Following this question was always the hovering memory of another poem, one that seemed to me to be totally in contrast to the mood of the de la Mare one – George Herbert's "The Banquet."

The Banquet*

Love bade me welcome; yet my soul drew back
Guilty of dust and sinne.
But quick-ey'd Love, observing me grow slack
From my first entrance in,

* Usually known as Love (III). The Banquet is a different poem by Herbert "Welcome sweet and sacred cheer".

Drew nearer to me, sweetly questioning,
If I lack'd any thing.

A guest, I answer'd, worthy to be here:
Love said, you shall be he.
I the unkinde, ungratefull? Ah my deare,
I cannot look on thee.
Love took my hand, and smiling did reply,
Who made the eyes but I?

Truth Lord, but I have marr'd them; let my shame
Go where it doth deserve.
And know you not, says Love, who bore the blame?
My deare, then I will serve.
You must sit down, sayes Love, and taste my meat:
So I did sit and eat.

So in addition to the feelings of weight and of being
supported, achieved by my "words made flesh" exercise, this
actual naming of the places where I was aware of the feeling
of support, from my feet upwards, had had another result;
it was that when I got as far as my floating ribs I at once
became aware of my breathing and its varying rhythm, not
interfering with it, not by doing it as a breathing exercise,
but just letting it happen, which added greatly to my sense
of joy in just being alive.

10

The incantation and "The Hidden Order of Art"

I now found myself back at that book I wrote in Spain with its record of my attempts to explore memories from my leisure activities that had the particular quality of feeling that I was later to call "beads." It was in the course of this study that I had found the preoccupations with Frazer's book *The Golden Bough* and the myths of the dying god. I also remembered how I had then invented for myself a certain silent incantation, saying "I know nothing, I want nothing, I am nothing," and discovered that after repeating it, whatever I was looking at took on a greatly increased quality of richness. Unable quite to believe in the usefulness of this discovery, I had not practised the formula when I got back to England and my everyday home and working life. I think I really forgot about it, even when the book was published (in 1938) and had one or two reviews by people who seemed to know what I was talking about. Then it was blitzed out of print during the wartime bombing of London.

Instead of remembering the incantation from Spain, I began intermittent Freudian psychoanalysis and also began to make doodle drawings (see Chapter 6) and had begun writing about them in a book that finally became *On Not Being Able to Paint*. It was not until many years later, in 1955, that I returned to consider the book I had made in Spain in 1936. It was when, at an International Psychoanalytic Congress in Geneva, I met Anton Ehrenzweig and told him about my experiment in leisure book. Soon he wrote a review of the book, calling it "The Creative Surrender," because that was what he thought the book was about.

During so many years since then, I have found myself asking, just what is it that has to be surrendered? Soon I began wondering whether William Blake might not be offering a clue when he says (using the world "annihilated" instead of "surrendered") "all that can be annihilated must be." But if this is so, just what is it that can be got rid of? Could it be the belief that anything good that one does is done only by what is called one's ego, that is, by one's own deliberative effort, consciously using rational thought? If so, must one be ready, intermittently, to surrender conscious "taking thought," and at the right moment letting the "not-known" have its say?

After writing his "Creative Surrender" review, Anton began the book called *The Hidden Order of Art*, and told me it was triggered off by his reading of my experiment in Spain, the emphasis in his book being on the word "Hidden," which for him certainly seemed to refer to his belief in a hidden ordering force, a way of thinking which, by its very nature, cannot be observed by everyday consciousness.

As for the idea of self-obliteration expressed in my incantation, I came to think of it in terms of the difference between conscious experience of separateness, and the feeling of borderlessness which can easily be feared as total non-existence, being nothing; a total emptiness, inside a void. Surely then my ability to use my incantation must require an ability to trust a hidden force making for order in one's self, for without this trust fruitful living cannot really happen. Does this not mean that I have constantly to trust a power that is totally more than anything I can achieve just by consciously willed endeavour?

But is not this what all my books are about? Is this perhaps what all the best of religious talk and ritual is really about, at least for me? Why then am I so cautious about remembering to use it, so unsure that it is safe to trust? Is it fear of all the awful things people do, saying that God told them to? Or does this only happen when they use the idea of God to sanctify their own egotism? Is it when what is said in their holy books is taken quite literally as the one and only truth so that anyone who does not agree, thus stirring their own doubts, must be done away with, murdered, burnt alive? Is this why I prefer not to use the word God, preferring the "I am" of the Hebrew Old Testament, But what does all this mean for me? I keep remembering "The TAO of which we speak is not the real TAO" (Lao Tze, 500 BC). And even our own Christian mystic, Meister Eckhart, with his insistence that "God is neither this nor that."

In short, I found Anton saying "It may seem strange that one should have to surrender one's surface functions, the very seat of one's rationality, in order to deepen one's sense of reality and truth." Yes, but again I wanted to add the word "intermittently" to the idea of surrendering the logical function, to add, not going for extremes, not trying to leave it out altogether, but allowing these two different states of mind to interact, interpenetrate, discovering their own rhythm of interchange.

All this about surface function now took me back to Jan Gordon in Los Angeles in 1928, and the subject of boundaries; and also to what I wrote in 1932, about being in the Black Forest in Germany. I now wanted to re-read it, because it had been so startling when it happened.

August 1930
The weather was wet and cold, my companion was nervously ill, so that we were prevented from following our plan of a walking tour, and, being unable to speak German, I had little wherewith to distract either of us from depressed brooding ... I was angry with my companion for being ill and angry with myself for being so self-centred as to grumble. I felt cramped that we must stay in a town, and my only delight was when the cold night air, blowing down our empty street, brought the smell of the encircling forest. I said, "If only the sun would come out then I could rest without thinking." And one morning I woke to find the sun was out and I went into the forest, wandering up a path to a cottage where they served drinks on little tables under apple trees,

overlooking a wide valley. I sat down and remembered
how I had sometimes found changes of mood follow
when I tried to describe in words what I was looking
at. So I said to myself, "I see a white house with red
geraniums and I hear a child crooning." This most
simple incantation seemed to open a door between
me and the world. I tried to write down what had
happened:

    ... Those flickering leaf shadows playing over the
heap of cut grass. It is fresh scythed. The shadows are
blue or green, I don't know which, but I feel them in
my bones. Down in the shadows of the gully, across
it through the glistening space, space that hangs
suspended, filling the gully so that little sounds wander
there, lose themselves and are drowned. Beyond, there's
a splash of sunlight leaping up against the darkness
of forest, the gold in it flows richly in my eyes, flows
through my brain in still pools of light. That pine, my
eye is led up and down the straightness of its trunk,
my muscles feel its roots spreading wide to hold it so
upright against the hill. The air is full of sounds, sighs
of wind in the trees, sighs which fade back into the
overhanging silence. A bee passes, a golden ripple in
the quiet air. A chicken at my feet fussily crunches a
blade of grass ....

    I sat motionless, draining sensation to its depths, wave
after wave of delight flowing through every cell in my body.
My attention flickered from one delight to the next like a
butterfly, effortless, following its pleasure; sometimes it
rested on a thought, a verbal comment, but these no longer
made a chattering barrier between me and what I saw, they
were woven into the texture of my seeing. I no longer strove
to be doing something, I was deeply content with what was.
At other times my different senses had often been in conflict,
so that I could either look or listen but not both at once. Now
hearing and sight and sense of space were all fused into one
whole.

    I do not know how long I sat there in absolute stillness,
watching. Eventually I stood up, stretched and returned

along the little path down the hillside, freed from my angers and discontents and overflowing with peace. But there were many questions to be answered. Which of the things I had done had been important in the awakening of my senses? Or was it nothing I had done, but some spell from the forest and the sun? Could I repeat the experience and so have a permanent retreat from the curse of my angers and self-pity? If just looking could be so satisfying, why was I always striving to have things or to get things done?

PART SEVEN

The family setting

11

My father, his breakdown and recovery

My father

In order to make clearer for myself what I might be trying
to do in writing this book, I now felt the need to write more
about my father. I knew that, having been the youngest child
in the large family of an Anglican clergyman in London, he
had been sent to Westminster School, where he claimed he
learned nothing. However, it seems he was chaired out of a
school concert for his singing a treble solo, a song called "The
Pilgrim of Love," or so I was told. On leaving school he was
sent via a relation to work in the London Stock Exchange as
a Stock Jobber. That he was totally unsuited for such work
is obvious to me now, for we had always been told that, at
the end of a week's work, he would set off walking alone into
the country, arriving at a friend's house for breakfast, with
a Shakespeare play in his pocket, and having recognised all
the different bird songs on his way. He was also a passionate
fisherman.

He married my mother in 1895 and for the first sixteen
years of his married life he daily set off for the city, wearing
a black silk top hat which I remember sometimes brushing
for him. Then suddenly in 1911, while getting dressed to go
to the train for London (we were staying with my mother's
parents in Fleet), he fell and hit his head on the iron
fireplace. He was only in bed for a week, during which time
none of us three children were allowed in to see him. When
I (aged 11) was allowed in, I saw the bruise on his head, but
all he said was, "How is Mickey?" i.e. our dog. This upset

me because he did not seem to know that Mickey had been left at our home in Guildford. When I then went out into my grandparents' field I met a woman from across the field, who had been called in to help my mother with the nursing. She also mentioned Mickey, so my father must have spoken to her too about him. I was suddenly angry that she was drawing attention to the fact that he was slightly confused about where Mickey was. (Mickey was an Irish terrier, older than me, and a very important member of the family.) This idea that our father might not be entirely in touch with actuality felt like the worst thing that had ever happened to me, and I remember crying and feeling angry with the woman for drawing attention to it.

For his convalescence he, accompanied by my mother, had gone fishing in Scotland, taking with them a male nurse, this having been insisted on by the consultant that he saw. I always used to think that this was fear he might fall again. I was left alone at home in Guildford, my sister being at boarding school and my brother a Naval Cadet at Dartmouth. An acquaintance of my parents came to look after me. During this time, I was one day hauled out of a gym class because they said I had a hunched left shoulder, which they diagnosed as curvature of the spine, but they did not suggest that anything could be done about it, except I must not play hockey and must carry my school satchel on my left shoulder. I was cross about the hockey, as I was due to be in the school team.

When my parents returned, I told my mother about this, crying a bit at the idea of having a crooked back, but this made her a little impatient, not surprisingly after all she herself must have been going through. I also told her that my dormouse had died and I had buried him in my garden, not telling the caretaker, who was offended when she heard about it, that I had not told her.

About this time, luckily for us, two of my mother's aunts died, leaving money to her and her sister, because, I was told, we were considered to be "not worldly," apparently unlike the other nieces. Thus my father, in 1917, was able to retire from the Stock Exchange, and we moved from Guildford to a village, Beacon Hill, on top of that dramatic great lump of hill, Hindhead, near Haslemere, which contains within its hump a deep valley called the Devil's Punch Bowl. The war was still on, so my father, for his war work, became the village postman. As he had never learned to ride a bicycle and was such a good walker, he was given the beat of going down into the Punch Bowl (no road, only a stony path in those days) where lived what were called the "Broom Squires," because they worked at making birch brooms. As these people were illiterate, he had the task of reading out to them the postcards from their sons in the trenches in France. He enjoyed all this greatly; sometimes, too, he had to deliver letters at the big houses on top of the hill, where my mother was often on calling-card terms, but the servants would sometimes ask him in for a cup of tea in the kitchen, which he talked about with much pleasure and amusement. He also taught himself to make beehives and kept, I think, twenty-five of them, until one year the bees all died of Isle of Wight disease. He also, on his long solitary walks, collected sphagnum moss, which, I was told, was used for treating war wounds in front-line hospitals. I can remember the lovely smell of it, drying in our house. Soon our local millionaire, having built a village club-house, and liking my father very much, asked him to be club secretary, which he became and remained until his death from cancer aged 55. At the time of the first elections after the war, he got out of bed to go to the village to vote Labour, having voted Conservative before the war.

I do not remember him ever being irritable after his retirement from the Stock Exchange, but I do remember him getting very upset when two people he knew in the village were having a quarrel, even though it was nothing to do with him. Also, when alone with me, he once said he was a failure and I, aged 19, (arrogantly?) said, "But you have had us." By this time I was at university studying psychology and physiology, and he once said, "I don't like your science," though he was soon to become very admiring of my brother, who was on the way to becoming a famous research physicist. Also, although he always liked to sing in the church choir, he once told me he felt like a kitten entangled in a ball of string, as regards his own beliefs.

It was my father who discovered and chose the place of our summer holidays. Beginning in 1904 we went every August for eight years to Bamburgh, Northumberland, with its superb castle on a rock rising straight from the sea-shore. It became a heaven for all of us children, meeting the same families who also came year after year, getting to know every rock pool and the creatures in it, while my mother happily did very good watercolour "sketches" as they were then called. (It was Jan Gordon who taught us to look on such activities as making pictures.) My earliest memory of my father, apart from the smell of his Harris tweed jacket, is his coming up to say goodnight to me, and singing the beginning of the hymn:

Now the day is over
Night is drawing nigh
Shadows of the evening
Steal across the sky
As the darkness gathers
Stars begin to peep
Birds and beasts and flowers
Soon will be asleep.

I have a last letter from him, written when he was already in bed, because of the cancer:

Dearest daughter,
Why are gulls called stupid? Your sketch of the gulls in the park and the waterhens' behaviour to them was good, I have often noticed that size does not go for much among birds as far as their treatment of each other is concerned. Bounce and cheek carry some birds a long way.

I have been watching the daily mystery and beauty of the dawn. The grey steals so quietly over the darkness and gradually creeps to the walls of my beautiful room almost shyly. The black bird wakes and immediately begins to scold some imaginary foe, wakes itself fully in the effort and then is its own good-tempered self again.

Alas not now does it lift up its priceless song. The hedge sparrow and robin both sing directly outside my window. The owls (little) were about some weeks ago but seem to have shifted their hunting grounds.

I have been reading an old favourite, "Homes Without Hands". Your copy it is. I did not merely read it when I was a little London boy, but I made it part of myself. Travelled to Africa on a moonlight night, saw the ungainly Ard Vark or anteater shuffle his huge paws over the Veldt and scoop a great hole in the ant heaps as one cuts a slice of a breakfast pudding. I would transport myself to S. America and see the humming birds etc. etc.

Life with me is now a game of hope and forward looking and yet a great peace withal. Nina* reads a lot to me. I think it is of great value to her to have all these tiresome things to do for me. Sounds egotistical, but she has time for reading and a little rest. I had a charming letter from Ursula† and she upbraided me for my writing, which she says wants a microscope.

All blessings on you, dear child
A.S.B.

* My mother
† A family friend.

12

My mother and us three children

Brighton

Probably at the beginning of my adolescence, my mother, perhaps half recognising my unspoken anger with my father on her behalf, had actually arranged for him and me to spend a weekend together, in lodgings in Brighton. During it we must have talked continually, though I cannot remember at all what about. Afterwards he said he had enjoyed it so much, adding, "I thought you were your mother's child."

At that time I had no idea what to make of this remark. It was only now, about eighty years later, when I was just beginning to write this book, that something happened that gave me a clue. It was when a colleague from abroad turned up, wanting to know about my family history. Amongst other things I had shown him a photograph of my mother and me standing together, she holding my hand. I think it must have been shortly before I went off to boarding school in Salisbury, aged 15. I had always disliked this photo, nearly throwing it away, I looked such a pudding-faced adolescent. But what my visitor had said was "Your mother really does look unhappy." I was greatly surprised that during all these intervening years I had totally failed to notice this. Very slowly, I began to face the possibility that my mother had been secretly unhappy, in her marriage, perhaps from the very beginning of my life. If so, could it be that it was not only my long-ago alligator kind of love that had produced the pain in her eyes? In fact I had to ask myself, had she been keeping her feelings dead so that it was not only J who had had to write about a kitten whose mother was dead? Did it not even make sense to try saying that I had somehow obliterated my intuitive awareness of my mother's unhappiness, something that she herself was doing? In fact it was not until she was somewhere in her eighties (she died at 91) that I had suddenly thought to ask her what had been the happiest time of her life. Her answer had been a shock to me. The background to this was the fact that long before this she had told me how, when first married and my sister was born, they lived in a cottage five minutes away from her parents' country house in Fleet. She now told me that her immediate neighbours had grumbled, "We know Mrs Blackett and Miss Blackett (my sister) but we don't know Mr Blackett." She had added that this was because he was always staying on in London, to go to sing in madrigal concerts. Yet here she was, in her eighties, telling me that this had been the happiest time of her life! I could not believe it, bearing in mind, as I always had done, many memories of what had seemed to me much happiness, especially on our year-after-year summer holidays in Bamburgh.

Having got so far, I now felt the need to look up my store of family photos and I happened on one of my mother actually holding her first born, my sister, and looking quite radiant with happiness; in fact, the only one among the many photos I have of her in which she looks like that. So I had to ask, what had gone wrong? Certainly, just as she seemed determined, via the prayer she gave me, to try to stop me speaking out in any way that might give offence, so she herself, I now realised, very rarely expressed anger, or even exasperation – except once, and this was only hearsay. It happened when we were living at Woking and news had come that my grandmother (at Fleet, a few stations away) had been taken ill. My mother had therefore taken the train to go and look after her, leaving us with my father in charge – or so she thought. As far as I can remember (I was about 5 at the time), we had suddenly found him opening our front door, ruefully remarking "It's the first time I have ever been called the last straw!" Apparently after my mother left, he had also taken the train to Fleet, going after her, and arriving at my grandparents' house only to have the door opened by my mother, who had burst out "Oh, but this is the last straw!"

Here I had to ask myself, was it that I had always been trying not to see my mother's pain and woes because of my not yet having properly separated out hers from mine? Which could have been what my father meant when he said he thought I was my mother's child?

As for that earliest pain that I must have seen in her eyes when I was sucking at her breast, it must have been different from any deliberate hurting. However I do remember, when I was perhaps aged 6, deliberately hurting, not my mother, but my sister, in a revengeful act. It must have been in the days just after starting the prayer, so I could not use words to express my anger at something my sister had done – perhaps snubbing me. What I had done was to deliberately and secretly smudge with my fingertips an ink drawing she had just done. There was one inadvertent causing of physical hurt to my mother, done in adult life out of my own sheer self-centredness. It was again when she was probably in her eighties and we were walking together to Kew Gardens from the underground station. She was rather slow, from age, thus undoing the moving too quickly of the rest of her life; I was now the one insisting on speed. So, thinking of a telephone call I could have made, I went back, quite unnecessarily, to the tube station to do it. When I returned, I found that she had tripped on a tree root in the path and hurt her hand; not seriously, but the scar always showed and made me feel guilty. I had now been forced to remember this because, years after her death, I myself had a phase of continual tripping and falling, injuring my shin, leaving grazes that were always very slow to heal. In fact, this phase of frequent falling had ended when I remembered the Kew Gardens episode. A belated victory achieved over Mrs Be-done-by-as-you-did, in fact a kind of forgiveness.

Us three children

Immediately after writing this about memories of my mother, I found myself in a state of deep gloom, full of doubts about the possible usefulness of this book; then, suddenly, comes a first memory of my mother as a whole separate person; I am making a daisy chain for her while sitting together on a grassy bank beside our lawn. But now there are twinges of misgivings. Granted I did love her very much, but what about the opposite feelings? Perhaps deflected onto my sister, as when I secretly smudged her drawing? This brings the thought that, in this book that I am now writing, there is very little use of the word "hate." J could cheerfully say that he hated Joyce and also tells of ideas of killing me. But what about my having been able to say to anyone "I hate you"? I am sure I must have said it to my sister, probably before I had to start saying that prayer? I do remember how, in our nursery squabbles, we were allowed to say "you beast" to each other but not "you fool," because doesn't the Bible say you will then be guilty of hell fire? Also it was about this time that I (probably aged about 6) developed what I called "one-eyed headaches" over my right eye, later labelled migraine. Even at the time I noticed that they used to come after I had been angry during a family meal, angry not with my mother or father, but with my sister since it was then that we were most often face to face and she could snub me. Eventually however I did manage to invent a non-verbal way of expressing my anger with my sister, in the form of a game which, because it was funny, I thought marked the end of our openly hating each other – or did it? It consisted of me slowly rising from crouching on the floor, slowly raising my head fully to face her, and then doing some dry spit. I called it "doing a cobra." I never had a migraine after leaving home to go to university.

Yes, but was this game really the end of the hate between us? It is true that subsequently we had very many years of close friendship, until she died of cancer in 1969; I being able to nurse her, she died in my own house. Her illness had come on nine years after her husband had died, nine years during which we had happily shared many activities. Only once, during all these years, had she suddenly exploded at me in rage, even her hands shaking, and looking as if she was struggling to control the urge to strangle me. Instead she had gone off out of the house and walked down the road trying to calm her fury. When she returned we never discussed what had happened, although I remember it had started with some practical problem about a ladder that we were trying to solve, and I had said "Wait a minute, just let me think."

Now I am remembering my angry hen collage, which reminds me that whatever internal god I was addressing in that prayer, I must have felt it was quite a powerful one, in that, ever since, I have been so afraid of offending with my tongue that I find it very difficult to begin speaking in public meetings. Recently, however, I have managed to say "shut up" to a friend and discovered that it did not give offence and she did shut up.

To go back to our early childhood years, it was in 1904 that our nanny left us, the one who admitted having spoilt me, though having been strict with the other two. At the same time, we also left the house (at Kenley, in Surrey), which had a lovely, flowery meadow and a little wooded copse, and moved into a smaller house in Woking with none of these things. Presumably the Stock Exchange was doing badly.

In adult life my mother told me that, after the nanny had gone, I cried for weeks and had diarrhoea. And my sister, also in adult life, said she remembers how terrible I was, that I cried if they even touched me. However, quite soon, a memorable day came when my brother and I discovered each other in playing together. Before this I had been envious that he, as a boy, did not have to do any housework, as I had to, helping to make the beds etc., so he had more time for play. I always remember secretly deciding (how mad can one be aged about 5?) that THEY had made a mistake, and that I was really a boy. I still had to help with the housework, but the memorable day came when he and I walked together along a sandy bank at the edge of a wood, playing at making bows and arrows. From then on, the closeness between us grew, to such an extent that, when I was about 18, my father said it was a pity we were brother and sister, we should really be able to get married.

Soon he did marry and we lost touch, he soon well on the way to becoming one of the most famous physicists of his generation. One memory stands out, from the early 1920s. We were walking together in Cambridge, and I quoted some rather mystical-sounding bit of poetry that I had liked in earlier years; he responded very coldly. As far as I can remember, the poem was by Francis Thompson:

When to the new eyes of thee
All things by immortal power
Near or far,
Hiddenly
To each other linked are,
That thou canst not stir a flower
Without troubling of a star.

But now comes a last memory, quite the opposite of that first happiness playing together. It is in 1973, when he, having been a Nobel Prize winner in atomic physics, made President of the Royal Society and a Lord in the Labour Government, is dying in the Middlesex Hospital. When I visit him there he asks, "Do you believe in prayer?" I think I said that I did not know what my praying could do in the outside world, but I did know what it does inside me. By this I think I meant a kind of holding the image of the person or activity I cared about, in stillness in my thoughts; an activity that does at least put a stop to the kind of nagging worry over feared catastrophe that I often indulged in, but which does nobody any good. I don't think he said anything in answer to this, I think those were our last words together.

As for my sister in adult life, she had won a place to go to Oxford University, when this was cancelled by the outbreak of the First World War. Instead, she learnt to become an extremely skilled cook in a convalescent home for war-wounded officers. After the war, she trained as an architect and built two houses, but gave up work when she married, becoming a splendid home-maker – being a skilled gardener, dressmaker and also piano player. She was very strong-minded, as is shown in a portrait of her (as Mrs Burger) by William Coldstream. It was actually his first ever portrait and is now in the Tate Gallery.

My brother, being already at Dartmouth Naval College when the war began, had carried on in the Navy throughout the war. After it was over, he was able to go to Cambridge to finish his education. While there he became excited by research physics, so resigned from the Navy to embark on atomic research. As regards his own memories, he once said in a public lecture that he had had "the kindly security of an Edwardian childhood."

After writing this I found myself playing the game of asking people about their first memories, so I had to face my own. It seemed quite preposterous, but it did look as if it had come from the house in London in which I was born. It is of me, quite naked and suspended in a black scarf, which is tied onto the hook of the spring scales that my father used to weigh the fish he caught, this itself hanging from the ceiling. The black scarf would be my sister's, since, according to photos, she would have been wearing a sailor suit, then the fashion for children, with its knotted black scarf in memory of the death of Nelson. I suppose that when fairly new born, I could have been weighed like that, though the "memory" must surely be a construction, because I seem actually to see this baby hanging there, so it must really be a dream. If it is a dream, what has this black scarf memorial for the death of Nelson got to do with me? What now comes is the day my mother called my father "the Last Straw," as well as a time I heard him say to her (rather ruefully) that she ought to have married a Highland Scot with a kilt and a red beard. Surely then, if my so-called first memory was actually a dream, on one level it could have been. It could have been registering the fact of us all being born into a family where my mother and father were secretly, even half unknown to themselves, battling with disillusion about their marriage, she desperately wanting him to be a hero, he very much aware of not being one.

13

Me being physically ill and the Undine story

The tail-less lizard

What happened next while remembering my parents' absence during my father's convalescence was that one image turned up again and again. It comes from the Nature

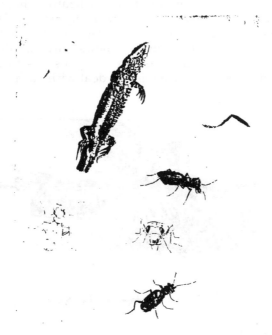

The tail-less lizard

Diary that I devotedly kept during adolescence. In amongst the many little drawings and paintings of birds, flowers, etc., I find a very precise ink drawing of a lizard without a tail that I had just seen, having once read that a lizard has the capacity to shed its tail when a predator catches it, intending to eat it alive.

One thing especially intrigued me about this drawing. It was that, just after looking at it, more than eighty years later, wondering just how the lizard did it, I had gone down to my sister's cottage in the country. There, out from under the summer-house darted a tail-less lizard. In all those eighty-odd years since drawing it, I had never seen another.

Two wild ducks and a drake

After wondering about this tail-less lizard, I happened to look again at the very first entry in my Nature Diary, for 1911, the one which says I had just seen two wild ducks and a drake. But the drawing shows only one duck, and my immediate thought was "So one of us has to go." As I have said, I seem to have tried to deal with such a triangle

Wild drake & two ~~dicks~~ ducks. Bramley. April 1st

Two ducks and a drake

problem by turning to Mother Nature; but I had also persuaded my brother to share my interest in Nature, so that together we explored looking for birds' nests and took photographs of them. However this does not seem to have been much of a way out of the two ducks problem, for, on reaching puberty, I became really ill, for the only time in my life so far. I missed a whole term of schooling because of being in bed with influenza, whooping cough and abscesses in both ears. I also grew as tall as I am now, all in one term. My parents even had to get a trained hospital nurse (in spite of the expense) to look after me.

What I chiefly remember about the illness is reading the German fairy-tale "Undine" in a borrowed copy of an edition illustrated by Arthur Rackham. It had what was to me then a wonderful picture of the wild girl from the lake standing on a hilltop in a storm, she herself directing the wind and the clouds by means of her water magic.

I was so caught by the story that when the book had been restored to its owner, and I was eventually off to boarding school in 1915, I took with me a little German edition I had found somewhere (being unable to find an English one), even though I knew no German and was not likely to be learning it.

Only now after all these years, do I ask myself why the story had so gripped me. To answer this, I tried a bit of free writing:

What about J's own first story, the wildness of the fox clashing with the cultivated life of the farmer? Surely the wild girl from the lake must really be a shut-away bit of me? Did my early having had to accept my mother's prayer mean I had had no hope of her ever becoming able to tolerate my wild Undine self and let it join up with the civilised part? But surely the prayer overdid the taming of the wild bit? I know I was a very good girl at school. Oh yes, except for that once, at boarding school, being caught trying to climb up a lamp post when we were all trailing back in line from somebody or other's Confirmation service in Salisbury's so lovely cathedral. Fortunately my house-mistress who had glimpsed me at it had a sense of humour. But could it not also have been that I was in general too good because of fear of an "Off with her head" Red Queen-Mrs Punch figure lurking in the wings of my inner stage?

In the Rackham edition is another picture of Undine as a sunny little girl just coming from the lake on to the doorstep of the childless couple who eventually adopt her. In the story she is described at first as full of pranks, which upsets her foster mother, though the father says he too has to put up with pranks – but from the lake.

The story tells how when Undine is 18 a wandering knight arrives from the forest, driven by the flooding of the lake, and Undine is captivated by him; so much so that when he tells his story of having been sent to the forest by a grand lady called Bertalda as a test of his love for her, Undine suddenly bites his hand. However, they soon become close and the foster parents arrange for them to be married and they set off through the forest to go to the Knight's castle and meet Bertalda. Though not consciously aware at the time of my adolescent reading of the story, I now noticed that it says that Undine was still wild and full of pranks after the marriage ceremony, but when she wakes from the wedding night, she is described as "so gentle." This seemed to fit with what she later told her husband, that Undines can acquire a soul by union with a human.

At first all goes well at the castle, but trouble comes when they all set out on a boating trip on the Danube. After an incident with Bertalda over some jewellery, Undine mysteriously disappears under the water, and the knight and Bertalda have to assume she is dead. Eventually a grand wedding between them takes place, but just as the knight is undressing and about to enter the nuptial chamber, a misty, veiled weeping figure emerges from the castle well and comes face to face with him. Her veil lifted, he sees Undine, "beautiful as ever," and he demands a last embrace, though she has told him that if he does it, he must die, which is what happens. As she leaves the room, she says to the waiting attendants "I have killed him with my tears."

The story ends with the knight's funeral, when again a veiled figure emerges, joining into the funeral procession, and finally turning into a spring which gushes out beside his grave, almost encircling it, says the story, thus embracing the husband in her loving arms. The spring finally flows away into the lake, a stream which the villagers say is still there.

As a child, reading this strange ending, I was quite mystified by the part played by a figure called Kulibore (said to be Undine's uncle) who has the power to turn himself into a flowing stream and cause the flooding of the lake. Also Undine says that it was this uncle who demanded that their last embrace will kill her husband with her tears. Reading this story now, I noticed how irritated I became by the fact that, after her wedding to the knight, at the fisher folks' cottage, Undine is always described as "so gentle," something which, considering the end of the story, does suggest that it is a story about a divided or split personality, the uncle being the split-off destructive part of Undine.

At the time of my illness my father was sufficiently recovered from his breakdown to be back at the daily grind of taking the train to London and the Stock Exchange; and sometimes, in the evening, he would come and sit in the door of my bedroom (not too close because of the whooping cough), just to chat, and with a wad of drawing paper given him for me by a friend at work. I am sure I did not talk to him about Undine.

Now, on re-reading the story for the purposes of this book, I began to wonder what had happened to that bit of Undine's personality that had bitten the knight's hand to stop him talking about Bertalda. Had she just grown out of such infantile kinds of jealousy? Or was it the fact that when a sea-maid unites with a human she acquires a soul? Perhaps it is this idea that the author of my version of the Undine story is trying to convey when he writes that after uniting with the knight she is always described as "so gentle." Considering the ending of the story I found the description rather inappropriate. Perhaps, instead of a soul, what she had achieved was a split in her personality, the not-so-gentle part finding a foothold in the figure of the uncle, Kulibore, who demands the knight's death through his embrace with Undine.

Undine controlling the weather

PART EIGHT

D.W. Winnicott and me

14

Being in analysis with
D.W. Winnicott

Although I began this book intending to avoid talking about psychoanalysis as such, I now found that I had to face the fact that there were certain questions I had never managed to ask in [any] one of my analyses.

What had happened was, first, that my training analysis, begun in 1939, was, I now think, rushed through, because of a shortage of analysts to take on the training of students, owing to many being away on war work. It was only after a few years of practising with patients that I happened to hear D.W. Winnicott (probably on a radio broadcast) saying that having swollen finger joints might have some connection with a bit of madness. Since I noticed my own finger joints had become swollen, I rang him, to say that I did not think my own training analyst had understood my mad bit, and could he advise me about who I should go to for some more analysis. After a little time (I don't remember how long) he actually suggested himself. Surprisingly, I accepted this without question, in spite of the fact that I was already analysing the patient that I have called Susan, who was actually living with the Winnicotts, he himself having sent her to me a short time before. He also suggested coming to do it in my house, since I lived half-way between his house in Hampstead and his consulting room in central London. I assumed he did this out of kindness, to save me time, since he knew that because my marriage had already broken up, I was trying to build up my own practice and pay for J's education. It seems I was grateful for this plan and, surprisingly, did not question the arrangement by which he was to be sitting daily in my consulting room chair, and me lying on my own analytic couch. He smoked while working, and one day after he had gone away at the end of a session, I found he had left behind, on a little table beside the chair, a most beautiful little crucifix, with the head of the Christ match bent right forward. Apparently I did not know what to make of this and did not mention it in my next session; I think I assumed it was something to do with his marriage, which I knew was childless, and vaguely thought could be unhappy. So I failed to ask, "Why did he do it?"

What I remember next is his first heart attack in February 1947. Shortly after, he phoned asking me to go and see him, he being in bed at home. He added that I was the first person he was asking to visit him. Of course I went, but all I remember is how small he looked in bed, with his wife Alice, rather a large woman, standing by. I do not remember what we talked about.

He soon recovered and, during the Easter holiday when I was at the Cedric Morris painting school in Suffolk, he suddenly dropped in to see me, having been taking leave of a friend at Harwich. He then told me of his meeting with Clare Britton, the psychiatric social worker whom he finally married. He was looking very frail and I was anxious lest he might have another heart attack. So, by now having heard something about his marriage problems, when he told me about Clare Britton I said, "If you don't leave Alice, I think you will die." He told me later that at that time he had not expected to return to work with me; however, soon he was back at work, though not in my house, as he had by now left his Hampstead home and was living alone in Queen Anne Street where his consulting room was.

During all this time, I was still working with Susan, who was extremely distressed by the break-up of their marriage, since she was very fond of Alice, who had originally rescued her from a mental hospital and brought her to live with them. She was by now so upset that she had had to leave the Winnicott house that she was taken in by a friend of theirs who lived close by. Being now unable to travel on her own, she was brought to me every day by taxi.

As for me, I quite soon found I could no longer manage the situation of having to analyse Susan in her temporary breakdown at the same time as being Winnicott's patient. Obviously I could not abandon Susan, so I left Winnicott and went for analysis to Clifford Scott, whose first comment was that it had all been a travesty of psychoanalysis. My analysis with Scott was very helpful, but in a few years he left to return to his own country. There had been very little said about sex in my time with Winnicott, but Scott talked much about it in relation to himself, finally saying, "If that is what you want, go and get it," which I did. Scott was also very helpful about one of my child patients (aged 11) who kept threatening to throw a brick through the playroom window. I had interpreted in fairly classic terms of her anger with me, with no effect. But Scott said, "I wonder, is it she perhaps wants to know if her first intercourse will hurt?" When I said this to her, she at once stopped threatening to smash the window.

Only recently, while sorting out my papers, I found a totally forgotten note, which says that, after I had given up analysis with Winnicott, we had a talk about the crucifix he had left with me. He said he knew he should not have done it, but that he would not have done it with anyone else. There is also a note on the sheet indicating my own thought at the time, that this being special was not what I really wanted, I wanted analysis.

Also in one of these chats he told me he thought I was a casualty of analysis, but added that anyway the period with him was far too short, lasting only four years. Apparently, once more I did not ask the right question, why had he offered himself as my analyst when he had Susan living in his house?

Now however, after all my work on the J diary and story book, I had a possible clue as to why he had done it. This clue came when I read Adam Phillips's book about Winnicott, which includes a poem sent by Winnicott to his brother-in-law, saying that it had come out of him and was very painful, and he hoped it would not happen again. Here is the poem.

The Tree

Mother below is weeping
weeping
weeping
Thus I knew her
Once, stretched out on her lap
as now on dead tree
I learned to make her smile
to stem her tears
to undo her guilt
to cure her inward death
To enliven her was my living.

This was a great surprise to me because, by now, I had read Clare Winnicott's introduction to the posthumously published collection of papers called *Psychoanalytic Explorations* in which she says "there is no doubt that the Winnicott parents were the centre of their children's lives, and that the vitality and stability of the whole household emanated from them. Their mother was vivacious and outgoing, and able to express her feelings easily."

While wondering about this contradiction of what the poem says, I suddenly thought again about the crucifix he had made and left with me, and began to think I might perhaps be able to understand a little more why he might have done it. Could it not be that the crucifix was an early version of the poem and that he, with his so great intuitive gifts, had, perhaps only implicitly, guessed that my problem could also be largely to do with a secretly depressed mother? Was it even possible that his poem was about something that had been left out of his own analyses? If so, here was something in himself which he did not yet know about consciously, yet unknowingly sought to find in analysing me. Thus the crucifix could have been his first attempt to bring it into consciousness.

But also, what about why I accepted his offer? Did I also choose not to think about the problem of Susan living in his house? Was I idealising him, after a long period of having been present as an observer in his Paddington Green clinic for mothers and babies, so that, for me, here was a father figure who understood about babies and their mothers? As well as that, he had blue eyes, was deeply musical, and able to be both funny and serious – all just as my father was. So could I have felt that here was someone I could get into communication with, talk to, in the way that I had failed with my real father, failed to communicate with him except for that one weekend in Brighton? I remember Winnicott saying, during my analysis, that I hated my father. Certainly I did remember how, as a child, I had hated my father for seeming to mock my difficulty in learning how to peel an apple. And when I was doing my piano practice, he would shout out "that's wrong!" when I already knew it was. I hated him for that, as well as for his irritability with mother. But I do not remember Winnicott saying that I also loved my father.

Certainly I remember that in my last session as Winnicott's patient, in 1947, I could not stop crying at having felt I must stop the analysis, just as I had been, according to my family, unable to stop crying when the nanny, who admitted having spoilt me, left us. What Winnicott did say seems to indicate that he was forgetting what Freud had discovered about how his patients transferred their feelings about childhood figures onto him. What Winnicott said to me, was that he did not know I felt so strongly about him.

The main interpretation that I remember he made was that I have been spending the rest of my life trying to deal with my father's schizophrenia. Was he right in what he said? Surely it depends on how you define the term schizophrenia? I do remember telling Winnicott that once, when we were living at Hindhead, my father, who sat at the head of the table in his Windsor chair, and was standing beside it just before a meal, suddenly bent over, put his hands on the arms of the chair, lent forward and kicked his heels up in the air. Winnicott said, "OK, if you thought it was funny (which I did) but it might have seemed a bit mad." He also said he thought my sister must have looked down upon me in my cot and hated me. It has taken me all these years to try to work out just what he meant by saying these things, in fact, to wonder if they were true. Certainly my memory of my father's game with his Windsor chair, trying to turn himself upside down, does fit in with the fact that at the beginning of my book *On Not Being Able to Paint* I was concerned with the discovery that when I had set out to do two landscapes, one of the peaceful Sussex Downs, the other of two huge beech trees, they had turned into their opposites: a raging heath fire and two tiny bushes in a blizzard.

As for the spine-like column I had seen in Winnicott's picture, I had at first thought it rather ferocious. So, since the father is generally seen as helping the baby separate from its mother, this picture certainly shows that, but suggests this did not happen gently.

Although my mother was a most predictable person both in character and devotedness, her breast abscess changed things. Then did this mean that I would never have any "continuity of being"? Was Winnicott right in using my first book as an example of my "for ever starting again"? I am still doubtful about this, for, as I see it, writing that book initiated change in my inner world that has been going on continuously ever since. Sometimes it occurs to me that his talking about a fresh start that never gets anywhere is his own wish to have actually been born a woman.

In fact my writing that book showed me that I am very glad to be a woman, and not the boy I had secretly thought I was. Did Winnicott's writing all those voluminous papers make him glad to be an analyst? Certainly we have his second wife's assertion that he did become potent in his marriage with her, but it was by then too late for her to produce a child. Does this link up with the fact of there being so little about fathers in his papers?

15

A Winnicott paper on disillusion about what one gives

I have only just discovered, while writing this last chapter, one of Winnicott's papers (also posthumously published in the collection of his papers called *Psychoanalytic Explorations* (1992). This one is called "Early Disillusion." Here are some short extracts from the paper, which is about a young woman patient, who had trouble with the use of her hands. Winnicott begins the paper by saying:

> Our patients, who teach us so much of what we get to know, often make it clear that they met disillusionment very early indeed. They have no doubt of this and can reach deeper and deeper sadness connected with this thought.
>
> The analysis proceeds, and yet a very great amount of work has to be done before the disillusionment can be described in words. Although there is no short cut to this result it is interesting to record individual results as they come.
>
> The complaint often is that the loved and idealised mother trained the child to be dishonest. Honesty seems to be something very nearly fundamental to human nature, and presently I shall say why I think it is not quite fundamental and how I think it can be analysed further. But whatever its origin there is no doubt that the little child – I was going to say infant – can get a bad shock from finding it is not good to be honest. How does it come about that the child is given to understand so early that honesty is not even the best policy, let alone good?

In two words, the baby lies there sucking her thumb and thinking thoughts, and someone comes and takes her thumb out of her mouth. She has to learn to get on with her thoughts without the obvious part of the orgiastic accompaniment.

It is quite clear that this patient cannot let her mother know that she masturbates with her hands, that her hands in the fantasy do steal and kill, and that she enjoys this to a degree. She does know that she enjoys destroying with her hands, and this knowledge goes right back to early childhood. But something is lacking in her ability to be honest and to let her mother know this through her masturbating. (She could always let her mother know by tearing up paper compulsively, or by upsetting things and making messes, i.e. defiantly.)

This woman is right at the end of her analysis, but cannot finish. One of her difficulties is this: that she can at last say, "thank you". She can at last believe she is grateful, but she cannot feel certain that I (her analyst) can accept her Gratitude fully. She can feel the whole thing in quite primary terms. She has been greedy at the breast, has loved it, pulled at it, torn it, scarred it, made it tired and old. Now she wants to give mother something. In herself she feels colour, value, life, but somehow she cannot believe in my acceptance of the perfect motion.

It is likely that in this case the mother really did contribute to the difficulty; not necessarily by taking the child's hands away from her genitals, but more likely by taking her tiny hands from her mouth and smacking them.

This young woman wants me to receive a gift from her inside, in return for what I have done. It is a perfect gift and she does not believe I believe in it. I don't.

The point is, that if I (her mother) cannot stand what in her honesty she tried to show me, when she was an infant, by her orgiastic activities, how can I stand the bad things which will certainly be there in the gift from her inside. In fact, a great chunk of good and bad fantasy material has been kept secret from me (mother), and as long as this is so she cannot be happy with her capacity to be grateful.

At first after reading this paper about secret attacks on one's mother, I thought what a lot of time it would have saved me if my analyst had known about it. However, once when leafing through my old notes, I found a sheet describing a session in which she does talk about just such imagined attacks that I must have thought I made on my mother. (I now think that my analyst had probably heard D.W.W. give the paper, perhaps the night before.) My note does not say that she thought I was doing these attacks on her, and as far as I can see now, this interpretation would not have had the slightest therapeutic effect on me, so this now seems to be an example of the truth that interpretations are of no use until the patient is ready for them. In my case, it had taken me another fifty years to realise just what I had to protect my mother from.

Apart from this, what especially interested me now was the theme of the wonderful "thank you" present that the patient wanted to give to D.W.W., one which he says he does not believe in any more than she does. Also the fact that he has chosen the word "Disillusion" for the title of the paper, but only once mentions anal gifts, described in terms of the hoped for "perfect motion." So here I found myself back on the theme of disillusionment at finding one's lovely gifts are thrown down the drain. Also that it could perhaps be especially important for people whose gift to the world is hoped to be via the making of "marks on paper" in various different ways.

A never forgotten memory from my childhood was stirred by the bits about thumb-sucking, and also about stealing from mother, for it reminds me of something I did at my first little primary school. It is of me sitting at a table with other girls, and sucking at a tiny pink pencil, moving it to and fro in my mouth. Suddenly it disappeared. One girl asked, "Didn't you swallow it?" I said "No," which was a lie. I never told anybody, but wondered what in the end happened to the pencil. It was the kind used for dance programmes in those Edwardian days.

16

D.W.W.'s doodle drawings

In 1995 a collection of Winnicott's doodle drawings was shown in London as part of a centenary celebration. When planning the exhibition, the organiser brought copies of them for me to see. Most of the doodles look like private jokes or caricatures of bits of himself or of other people, many of them taking the form of strange animals. But there is one that is quite different, a mother and baby. An abstract simplified form of it was printed on the brochure of the Winnicott Celebration in Milan in 1997. The one shown here, a reproduction of the original, has this black central column, making it impossible to see the contact of the mother and baby's bodies, though the baby's beautifully drawn left arm is shown as if holding on to the mother's neck. Whether it is actually supporting her, or hanging on to her for dear life, is not clear – perhaps both. The baby's feet are also beautifully drawn and tucked under its bottom, but the mother's right forearm and hand, which should be supporting the baby's feet, are shown as having lost all solidity, and a gap is left between her arm and the baby's feet.

There are at least three versions of this drawing; the second was used on the cover of the book by Jan Abram entitled *The Language of Winnicott* (1996). In this one, the baby's feet and the gap between them and the mother's non-existent hand is blacked out, scribbled over. Also in this version, one of the mother's breasts is clearly shown, but the left one is almost indistinguishable from the baby's bottom.

A third version occurs in Robert Rodman's book of Winnicott's letters, called *Spontaneous Gesture* (1987), and here the mother's and baby's faces are not blotted out by the black column and are shown as slightly apart, with the baby's left arm clearly shown. I noticed that in all three versions Winnicott has put a shape almost like ribs emerging on both sides of the central black column which

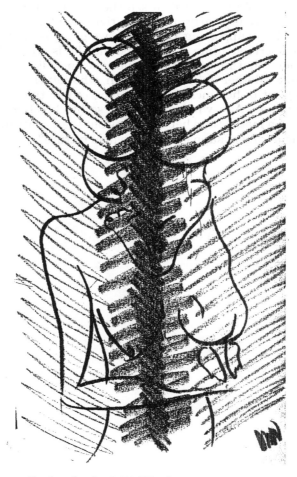

Doodle drawing by D.W. Winnicott

itself goes right down to where the mother's pelvis should be, but is not shown; it also goes right up above her head. These black rhythmic lines on one side point downwards and on the other side go upwards, as if representing the rhythm of breathing?

Just what is D.W.W. trying to work out in these three drawings of a mother and a baby? Apart from the black column making it hard to see the actual contact between them, there is clearly shown the right hand and arm, which should be supporting the baby's weight, just fading away into a scribbled line. Could it be that he is struggling with the idea that his internal mother does not like his bottom? (Unlike Mother Julian of Norwich, who felt that God loved every bit of her including that part of her that she called her purse.) And what about that so black column coming between mother and baby, blotting out their contact, yet also being a kind of support for the whole picture?

PART NINE

Towards wholeness

17

Towards bringing bits of one's self together

I have just been glancing through some of my quite recent doodle drawings, made in 1993, and find one that, although it meant nothing to me at the time, now insists on being attended to. What it first says to me is "A man can smile and smile, and be a villain." Presumably it's a bit of me, but what sort of villain? The word that comes is "treachery." To what? To the truth of my own experience? My terrible need to comply with people, be in harmony, avoid disagreement? But what else does it say? Those two lumps on each side of the top of its head look like incipient horns. But its one eye seems to twinkle at me (cf. J's story of the boy on the boat called Bobby Twink). Now I see those lumps on its head, not as incipient horns but as the ears of my childhood teddy bear, that I called "Chumps." But his smile has pretty savage-looking teeth, pointing down to those horizontal lines that look like fingers. This reminds me of recently becoming aware of a kind of blocked feeling in my fingertips. Could this be a memory of having one's fingers smacked for using them enjoyably to explore one's own body? In fact I have only one actual memory of being smacked and that is by my mother for not tidying my chest of drawers, she herself being a very tidy person. But the smack did not have the desired effect, not even now.

What then about the "smile and smile, and be a villain"? The memory that comes is painful. It is that back in Guildford just after my father's breakdown I had gone to tell my best friend and her mother about it. I said that my father had been very ill. They had looked suitably shocked, but I had been aware that I was smiling when I told them. But why? Was it a case of trying to protect myself against woe? Or was it something more sinister? Was it a feeling that he had been paid out, that I had got my revenge for his mocking, as I felt it to be, at my struggle to peel an apple? Doesn't this fit with my flash of feeling myself to be Hamlet's father's ghost, full of ideas of taking revenge? Yet K who has also seen this drawing says there is a certain warmth in it. Certainly in so far as it is Chumps, my teddy bear, there must be warmth in it, he did give me much comfort. But what did it actually mean, when I gave him the name of "Chumps"? Did it really mean that I already knew what a chump I was to think that perhaps I was really a boy and that "they" had made a mistake; had I been chump enough to deny the evidence of my own eyes?

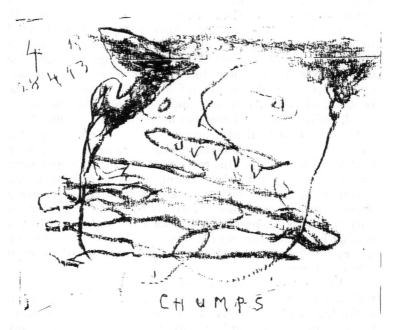

Chumps

The three faces

While thinking such thoughts, another of my doodle drawings turned up, probably made some years before at the same time as the Chumps one, but ignored because I had not liked the look of it. Now I see it as three profile faces placed on three sides of a rather square-shaped head. I thought the profile faces must be different aspects of me, in which case the squareness could indicate something hopeful, a move towards wholeness?

The profile facing the left side of the paper has a sharp pointed nose and its lips firmly held together as if shut – to avoid offending with its tongue? But from its throat a line goes right across to the second profile, facing the other way and placed lower down on the back of the head's neck. In this one the tongue is clearly shown and it has an avid look. I also see that the lower outline of the tongue is extended to form another shape, which looks like the end of a broken bone. Is this to do with how destructive a mouth can be, even saying words can cause a death? The face lying on top of the head has a wide-open mouth and also a wide eye staring upwards. The open mouth looks to me as if it is crying out in pain, and the staring eye has what looks like a tear falling below it. I could now try out seeing it as depicting me as a baby, lying on my mother's lap, looking up into her eyes and seeing pain there, and not knowing whose pain it is because she and I are not yet felt to be separate. Its staring quality is perhaps the most important thing for me in this drawing. It reminds me that, of recent years, I have been discovering that a change of mood, from a vague kind of depression, can be brought about simply by bringing nearer together the upper and lower eyelids; it seems to bring with it a cheerful acceptance of one's own separateness, such a simple movement, but it seems to free me from compulsive agreement and compliance, making difference and therefore separation acceptable.

I am reminded of my angry hen collage, and the thought that whatever internal god I was addressing in that prayer, it was quite a powerful one, in that ever since I had been so afraid of offending with my tongue that I find speaking

The three faces

in public meetings very difficult. Recently, however, I have managed to say "shut up" to a friend and discovered that it did not give offence or break the relationship, and she did shut up.

Satan and a burst blood vessel?

It was soon after writing about my analysis with Winnicott that I woke one morning to find that something odd had happened to my sight. I noticed that the vertical lines of whatever I was looking at, for instance the upright parts of a window frame, had gone crooked or slanting, while the horizontal lines were straight.

Totally bewildered by this, I called in on my local optician, who sent me off to an eye clinic, where I was told

I had burst a blood vessel in my left eye, but that it would get better, though after getting a second opinion, they said it would not. Nothing was said about what might have caused it, so I began asking myself just what had happened the day before. What I had been doing was attending a lecture in which there had been shown one of William Blake's original engravings for his book *Visions of the Book of Job*. It was the one showing Job's nightmare, with Satan, the rebel angel, hovering over Job's prostrate body; Job and Satan both have the same face, just as Job and God the Almighty have the same face in the first picture in the series.

It seemed then that I had to face the possibility that it was my own secretly rebellious Satanic self that might have caused the bursting. Probably experts in the physiology of the eye would say that's all nonsense, it must have been some passing increase in blood pressure. But what about anger? Doesn't ordinary speech say "I was so angry I could have burst a blood vessel"? And there was something else about the Job picture: it was that Satan's outstretched body is shown lying very close to Job's, with only a narrow gap between them. So it could be that what had sparked off my eye burst was a terror that a split-off and angrily rebellious bit of myself would emerge with disastrous results. But why an eye burst? Could it be that a bit of me felt that to burst an eye blood vessel, which happens silently, is safer than to burst out with Satanic rebellious speech?

Such an idea took me straight back to the Undine story and suddenly I now could see it in terms of a split in her personality. When she first comes from the lake, she is described as being full of pranks and mischief, but after she is married to the knight, she is always described as so gentle. It was this constant use of the words "so gentle" that irritated me in the English version of the story (which says it is taken from a French account of the original German folk tale).

Suddenly I could see a new aspect of my Satanic rebellious self, shown in an extreme inhibition of my ability to read my own handwriting, though I could still read typescript. More and more I could feel myself behave as if I were saying, "Why should a letter be that shape not a

Blake engraving

different one?" (you, who said, cheerfully, mockingly, "You want to create your own alphabet").

The squashing down head

Yet another of my doodle drawings now turned up, I think from the same batch as my "Chumps" one. I did not like it much because of the flat horizontal edge of the top of the head. But now I saw that this top-of-the-head form was made up of circular forms all squashed together, with not a single line going upward. It seemed to be a caricature of my compulsive agreement tendency. But down below is this little dark dancing figure rather like a young animal, its exuberance being in total contrast with the flat top of the head.

The thought that came was Blake's "little creature made from joy" and "mirth," but, from the way my mother, at the beginning of my puberty, tried to tell me about the facts of sex, I do not think there can have been, for her, all that joy and mirth in the making of us three. I don't know if she had enjoyed being pregnant as much as I had with J. However, I do know she had enjoyment when we were actually in the outer world.

I do not know who first wrote the phrase "the intolerable compliment of the love of God" though I do remember that I found myself silently saying it just after a very good love-making.

The squashing down head

18

The Easter story: the need for fiction

As a result of my eye burst, I could no longer read the titles of the books standing on my shelves, so sometimes I would pick out one at random and see what it might have to tell me. Today what came is what looks like an old number of a small Catholic journal called *Blackfriars* (no date on it). I remember it was given to me, eight or nine years ago, by an ex-Jesuit priest turned psychotherapist. Not being a Roman Catholic myself, I had not given time to read it then, but now, although battling with my eye trouble, I have managed it. It is titled *Catholic Faith and Easter Stories: Reflections on Hubert Richards* and is written by an eminent Jesuit priest and lecturer in philosophy, Fergus Kerr OP. Here is a passage from it.

With the recent publication of *The First Easter*,[1] Hubert Richards has presented Catholics with problems about the literary status of the resurrection narrative. He says that "The questions that are being asked of the resurrection today may shatter some of our most treasured assumptions". He anticipates that his interpretations will seem strange and shocking, and that some will doubt whether he believes in the resurrection of Jesus at all. It is, however, precisely his deep faith in

[1] Hubert J. Richards, *The First Easter: What Really Happened*, London: Fontana, 1976.

the resurrection of Jesus at all. It is however his deep
faith in the resurrection that impels him to try to lead
his readers "from the superficialities to the heart of
the matter". How many of us realise in any detail how
different the four accounts of the Passion are from one
another; and how illuminating for our faith the contrast
is? Don't most of us, believers and non-believers, take
it for granted that we know what the resurrection of
Jesus is about? Don't we take it for granted that we
know what the Easter narratives mean? Don't most of
us, believers and non-believers, assume that faith in the
resurrection involves, and even depends on, treating the
Easter narratives as essentially historical accounts of
meetings that the disciples had with a dead man who
had been "raised" (in effect resuscitated and reanimated)
"from the dead", and was able to appear and disappear at
will, pass through closed doors, display scars for them to
finger, barbecue fish, and so on, all of which is assumed
to demonstrate the power of almighty God ...

As Hubert Richards points out, however, the stories
in the concluding pages of the gospels do not provide such
a clear and coherent account as we generally imagine:
"as literal descriptions of what took place, the stories are
quite incoherent and totally irreconcilable" and, he adds,
"the stories were never intended as literal descriptions of a
sequence of events and should not be treated as such." When
the Easter stories are compared with one another, it proves
impossible to resolve the contradictions and discrepancies.
Mark manages to refer to the resurrection without narrating
any appearance story; Matthew places a final appearance
of the risen Christ in Galilee, whereas Luke seems to shift
it to Jerusalem. Paul seems never to have heard of the
empty tomb that occupies a place in all four gospels. In
short, Richards concludes that "there is no one coherent
or consistent or exclusive account of the resurrection
of Jesus."

Richards proceeds to show how the Easter narratives
developed, and how ways other than the language of
"resurrection" of putting the Easter experience into words

existed from the outset. Most of us assume unthinkingly that the gospels are earlier than the letters of St Paul, simply because they come first in the book. It is certainly a widespread assumption that the gospel accounts of the resurrection are much closer to the original event than anything in St Paul. Anybody with the slightest acquaintance with the chronology of the New Testament writings knows that precisely the opposite is the case; but even then doesn't the idea linger on, against what scholarship has proved beyond argument, that the apparently simple and naïve testimonies of these people who walked and talked and ate with Jesus after he had risen from the dead are much nearer in time to what happened than the various accounts of St Paul's experience on the road to Damascus?

It is very striking, however, when one puts the Easter narratives into the chronological order in which they were composed, to discover that the earliest are by far the most reticent and uninformative. The later an account is in the history of the formation of the Easter narrative, the more likely it is to be detailed and circumstantial; the further a writer gets from the event, the more he seems able to say about it. In the early 50s Paul says simply that the risen Christ appears to him, and in the earliest of the gospels, Mark communicates his faith in the resurrection without mentioning any appearances at all. In the late 70s, however, Matthew writes of the risen Christ appearing to the eleven on a mountain in Galilee and delivering a discourse of stupendous significance. Ten years later, Luke tells the story of a Christ who joins two of his disciples on the road, and, remaining anonymous, expounds the scriptures before sitting down to share a meal with them. Finally, perhaps in the closing decade of the century, the Christ of John's gospel invites doubting Thomas to finger his scars, and in a kind of epilogue makes a fire and cooks breakfast for the disciples. As Hubert Richards remarks, "stories that grow like this in the telling need to be taken as stories, not as history."

The shift from Paul's received declaration (e.g. I Corinthians 15:8) to the expansive, picturesque and detailed narratives in Luke and John is very striking. Consider how

the first half of the story goes in the King James version, in
Luke 24:13–27:

> And behold, two of them went the same day to a village
> called Emmaus, which was from Jerusalem about three
> score furlongs. And they talked together of all these
> things which had happened. And it came to pass that
> while they communed together and reasoned, Jesus
> himself drew near, and went with them. But their eyes
> were holden that they should not know him. And he
> said unto them, What manner of communications are
> these that ye have one to another, as ye walk, and are
> sad? And the one of them, whose name was Cleopas,
> answering said unto him, Art thou only a stranger in
> Jerusalem, and hast not known the things which are
> come to pass there in these days? And he said unto them,
> What things? And they said unto him, Concerning Jesus
> of Nazareth, which was a prophet mighty in deed and
> word before God and all the people. And how the chief
> priests and our rulers delivered him to be condemned to
> death, and have crucified him. But we trusted that it had
> been he which should have redeemed Israel .... Then he
> said unto them, O fools, and slow of heart to believe all
> that the prophets have spoken. Ought not Christ to have
> suffered these things, and to enter into his glory? And
> beginning at Moses and all the prophets, he expounded
> unto them in all the scriptures the things concerning
> himself.

The "And behold" there might be taken as a signal to the
listeners or readers to whom Luke addresses himself to use
their imaginations – to visualise the two disciples making
their way from Jerusalem back into the country. The village
of Emmaus has never been successfully identified. As Kerr
writes, the irony of having the unidentified Jesus asking for
information about what had happened to himself prepares
us for the mere recital of the bare facts which the disciple
finally vouchsafes.

Instead of being a naïve report of one of the earliest
appearances of the risen Christ, this narrative is surely

a very sophisticated parable accounting for the rise of the Christian interpretation of the scriptures. There can be no doubt whatever that Hubert Richards believes in the resurrection of Christ; he has no objection, he says, to being told that his understanding of the resurrection is different from someone else's. He has no desire to impose his interpretation on others as the only possible one. Indeed, his point throughout the book is that there is, and always has been, a variety of ways of interpreting what happened to Jesus when he went to God. The question is not of imposing a new orthodoxy, but of exploring what liberty a Catholic has to treat the Easter narratives as a special kind of fiction. Some pages by Brian Wicker in *The Story-Shaped World* surely put one on the right road. Under the pressures of a culture such as ours has been for centuries, in which narratives have been separated out into either the empirical or the fictional, it may have been inevitable that the gospels should have been read in a uniformly literal mode.

Of course, this mention of the word "fiction" takes me back to J's story book with his inventions in the space on top of the chimneys. Not only this, but my own collage that had called itself "The Listeners," and that had been seen, by an ex-priest turned psychotherapist, as depicting the story of the walk to Emmaus. Also my own having happened to notice, on going to Jerusalem, that there was no such place as Emmaus marked on the map.

19

An area for the
play of opposites

Before discovering this essay by Fergus Kerr, I had written
a chapter about J's use of the space on top of the chimneys
in the Station Hotel picture and the fact that he had put
a religious symbol in the space. After trying to collect my
thoughts on the subject, I found myself searching the D.W.W.
writings to find out when he himself began writing about
such in-between spaces as were used by J's picture. In the
end I found that it was in 1951, as far as I know:

It is generally acknowledged that a statement of
human nature is inadequate when given in terms of
interpersonal relationships, even when the imaginative
elaboration of function, the whole of fantasy both
conscious and unconscious, including the repressed
unconscious, is allowed for. There is another way of
describing persons that comes out of the researches
of the past two decades, that suggests that of every
individual who has reached the stage of being a unit
(with a limiting membrane and an outside and an inside)
it can be said that there is an inner reality to that
individual, an inner world which can be rich or poor and
can be at peace or in a state of war.

My claim is that if there is a need for this double
statement, there is need for a triple one; there is the
third part of the life of a human being, a part that we
cannot ignore, an intermediate area of experiencing, to
which inner reality and external life both contribute. It
is an area which is not challenged, because no claim is

made on its behalf except that it shall exist as a resting-place for the individual engaged in the perpetual human task of keeping inner and outer reality separate yet inter-related.[1]

Here is a theoretical statement of something that for me goes right back to 1959 and J's use of the spaces on the chimney tops.

Realistically, they are where cowls are sometimes put to control the smoke, keep fires from smoking into rooms. J had evidently decided intuitively that here was a place where there could be room for the play of invention.

In fact his father, having an engineering degree and being an inventor by temperament, was always, when well enough, constructing new technologies that were much ahead of their time though he never managed to market them. For example, shortly before J's stories were written, Dennis had been making a new kind of sailing boat, built on our back lawn and actually launched on a large North London lake, only to have it abandoned when the war came.

Hence invention was very much in the air of our household. When I asked J (he now being nearly 60) about the contraptions on the chimney tops, he said he thought they were stimulated by seeing Louis Wain's cat pictures, though I could see nothing cat-like in them. As for the particular shapes he uses, the first one, which appears on the house opposite the story of the kitten whose mother was dead, is in the form of a grid, which is in fact realistic; cowls on chimneys were sometimes shaped like that. But might he not be using its shape for the symbolic value of its black and whiteness? If so, it could provide a diagram of what may be the most primitive first attempts to find order in one's earliest experience of being in the world, that is in extremes of either-or-ness, black or whiteness, bad or good. Here I remembered how Freud talked of this in terms of what is to be spat out or to be swallowed. In fact the grid

[1] *Transitional Objects and Transitional Phenomena* [1951], in D.W. Winnicott, *Collected Papers*, London: Tavistock Publications, 1958.

does not appear again until the porter story, on top of the first one of the three chimneys on the Station Hotel; and next to it is the shape I have already seen as looking like a chalice (or an egg cup?) held within what could be the horns of a crescent moon; while the third chimney has a similar shape, but less chalice-like and more like an egg half held between the horns of the moon; the curve of the moon-shape is now supported by what look like human legs, with two tiny feet pointing away from the station, towards the railway lines.

The space between inner and outer

Further, I have considered how all these inventions, what-ever their exact meaning, are placed in the half-way area between the inner world of the hotel and the otherness of the outside world, of the real world, a half-way area where J apparently felt free to play with shapes from the outer world and use them for his own purposes.

Continuing to think about these contraptions on the chimney-pots and the fact that he had put them in this half-way space, I was now taken in memory right back to our days in Los Angeles, when Jan Gordon had talked to us on the subject of outline as being, visually, the most unnatural thing in nature. Also how I had soon after seen two jugs placed close together and had set out to draw them, only to discover to my surprise that the outlines did merge.

It even occurred to me now to consider whether J's use of this in-between area for his play with images might not correspond with my original excitement in finding that the man who was going to ask me to marry him could play with the depiction of smoke from the engine in the quarry, a capacity for visual play which (perhaps unwisely) had influenced my subsequent decision to marry him.

About twenty or so years after drawing the two jugs, and after many years working as a psychoanalyst, one of my patients had produced a large number of spontaneous drawings, some of which contained overlapping circles. These had reminded me of my two jugs drawing, and gave me the idea of what a useful diagram it provided for thinking about this space of overlap between what comes from the private inside of one's self and what is there in the shared world outside.

The in-between space and sacredness

In this connection I had been particularly interested that J's play in the in-between area had produced the markedly religious symbol: what looks like a chalice. I therefore returned to J's ideas about what he called God, in relation to this shape in the in-between area. Whether or not he had heard anything about the Christian ritual where the wine in the chalice is looked upon as the blood of Christ, I do not know. The fact that he had put a cross on each of the lighthouses in the first bridge picture did suggest that he might be struggling, amongst other things, to express something to do with an idea of sacredness, especially since, in the diary, there are notes about his so frequent play of making what he called "cathedrals" out of odd bits of wood. Did this mean that it was J's bit of each man's poetic genius that had prompted him to put the chalice form into the chimney-pot area, because this part of him already knew that this particular kind of in-between space is where religious creeds and rituals belong?

The chalice, and having his own feet

At the same time there was no doubt that I had to think of the chalice as linked with the idea of his having, over the years and beginning with his breastfeeding, achieved an image for an inner source of goodness, maybe idealised and made sacred, in order to keep it safe from becoming the bitten-into moon? If this was a useful way of seeing it, then it did look as if he is coming to believe that he now has enough inner resources to enable him to have his own feet, and not just in the direction of the fun of having his own tent but in the direction of work, as done by the devoted porter. Perhaps, in the stories, he has portrayed his hope that he is eventually going to be able to combine both work and fun, for by the time I was writing this book he told me that this was now true, that he was finding that his work was fun.

The swing of the tides

Still continuing to brood about the shape that might be a chalice there came the idea of how cups are useful because of their capacity for being sometimes full and sometimes empty. A cup that is always full would become stale, so emptiness is recurrently necessary if it is to be a filling with something new, something fresh.

This now took me back to one of the most notable elements in the two bridge pictures, the addition of the two words "wet" and "sand." It suggests that there was here something very important to him, but that he knew no other way of drawing attention to it except by words, the something being the sway of the tides under London's bridges. So I asked myself, is it so important, both to him and to me, because he is aware of the swings of feeling within himself, times when he could feel the fullness of life within him, other times when there is a sense of inner loss, even of total emptiness? But he had certainly dealt with the emptiness creatively in the stories by using his active hand and his imaginative eye when facing the empty bare sheets of the exercise book.

The sea-shore of endless worlds

Suddenly now, thinking of the space-between area of his chimney tops, I remembered how in adolescence during the First World War I had read Rabindranath Tagore's book *Gitanjali*, and had been haunted by the phrase "on the sea-shore of endless worlds children play." Also I had often been surprised that the lines of poetry that now seemed most special to me, out of all I had ever read, were Shakespeare's:

Come unto these yellow sands,
And there take hands:
Courtsied when you have and kiss'd
The wild waves whist.

Only now did it strike me that it was in the space
between the high tide and the low tide, the place of meeting
of the opposites of the politeness of the formal dance, with its
courtesy, and the wildness of the waves, that new things can
happen: the endless worlds of the sea-shore of children's play.
So also J's story book was his play, done in the boundaried but
unstructured empty space-time given him by the school; and
using the memories of what he had encountered in the outside
world, together with all his own feelings about the encounters.
He had shown how these continued to exist, in the form of
images, conscious or unconscious, developing within him,
all giving shape to his hopes, fears, anxieties and longings.
Central to these seemed to be his queries about what sort of
goodness there is to be believed in and trusted to support him
through all the joys, sorrows, mysteries, of being alive.

Emptiness and "O" and God

There was no doubt that J had made good use of the empty
space and time he had been given by his school, but what
about other kinds of emptiness, such as the loss of feeling
there is any point in going on living, or the state of emptiness
of meanings of words or images, no ways of telling what is
really happening either inside or in the outer world, not to
mention the emptiness of a loved person not being there
when they ought to be? Then I remembered that once in the
diary J had asked about the letter O as meaning "nothing"
and this reminded me that I had, several years ago, quoted
Meister Eckhart's use of the word "Godhead" as "that which
contains all distinctions as yet undeveloped and is therefore
darkness and formlessness."

So here it seems it was necessary to have another look
at the positive sides of emptiness, of not-knowing, of being
in the dark, for J had certainly at times found something
alluring about darkness, as in the tunnel on the Heath
where he said his wolf goes in. Could it be that he was there
trying to say something more than just anal curiosity and
excitement, something more than wanting to know about
the unseen innerness of the body, and where he came from;
in fact, something about innerness in general?

Stillness and the winds of the spirit

Incidentally, I had already noticed how the smoke from the steamer in the first bridge picture goes straight up, unlike the smoke from all the houses, thus suggesting that it is a completely calm windless day. Could this be perhaps a moment of great peace even achieved by this joining together of the two lighthouses, standing both for parents and also aspects of himself, by the wire rope and the lanterns. It is interesting that on the second lighthouse picture, which shows only the tallest lighthouse and celebrates the lighthouse keeper coming down to join in the game of dominoes, the cross has been replaced by a weather vane and on top of this is a shadowy cock, high up and safely out of danger from foxes. The addition of the weather vane suggested also an ability to sense which way the wind blows, both in the family situation and in the wider world of "the people" who thought the dominoes game on the boat was "great fun." There was also to be considered the winds of change within himself, not only the winds of the spirit, but I remembered as well that outer world winds had quite often been important in the diary. There was one which was of J coming down early one Sunday morning, after poking his head out of his attic window, and saying, "There is a quiet country wind."

Making a spirit stove

Further, I have considered how all these inventions, whatever their exact meaning, are placed in the half-way area between the inner fire of the hotel and the otherness of the outside world, of the real world, a half-way area where J apparently felt free to play with shapes from the outer world and use them for his own purposes.

Continuing to think about these contraptions on the chimneys-pots, and the fact that he had put them in this half-way space, I was now taken, in memory, right back to our days in Los Angeles, when Jan Gordon had talked to us on the subject of outline being, visually, the most unnatural thing in nature.

Conclusion: Useable dreams

Most of these dreams were not written down, only remembered, and so are mostly not dated and not in chronological order.

The road to Deal

Once (at the beginning of writing this book) I dreamt that my path which usually went over rather desert places now took me through the back garden of an imagined cottage belonging to my retired training analyst, I was asking her the way, she pointed to the steep grass embankment beside the garden, on top of which was a main road leading to Deal.

Free thought: Why Deal? I once went to Deal to paint again a picture I had made there that had been sold at my 1971 exhibition. But the street that I had painted had gone. So I had lain down instead on the beach. The waves' rhythm made me aware of my breathing.

The walls of Jericho

Another dream (quite recent – 8 September 1997): Still on the usual sandy path I find my way forward is blocked by a pile of fallen masonry. When trying to get through it I find myself standing on a wobbly bit of it.

Free thought: "When Joshua hit the City of Jericho and the walls came tumbling down." It looks as if I am having to give up a defence against something in myself, but also be very careful not to fall over physically. However after a few weeks I did fall and have a weekend in hospital.

The three planks

Some months ago I had a dream, I was struggling along a very steep muddy bank just above an expanse of equally muddy water. All that kept me from slipping into it was having my feet on three ledges, also muddy, but they supported my feet till I got beyond the bank, onto firm land, and was walking towards some shop, perhaps a chemist. Somebody seemed to be beside me and said "Ought you to be doing it by yourself?" I said "Yes, that's OK. I always do."

Free thought: The first thoughts that came were that the ledges that support my feet on the slippery bank are my three Joanna Field-type books that look for beads of memory. Slipping into thickly muddy water sounds like depression, terror of being swept away, drowned. But the bit about "always doing it myself" seems to link up with my recurrent awareness of holding my lower jaw rigid, a kind of inability to let go, unable to trust any support.

And this is in total contrast with all those A.A. experiences I had had. But then comes the question, just what is it that one does have to do, oneself, if anything fruitful is to happen, what does one have to attend to find that trust, which is the question that I have been trying to answer in the whole of this book.

So is not this dream really about my struggle to trust the A.A., the answering activity, or whatever one chooses to call this something that I knew from experiences does need to be trusted, in spite of its being so hidden. Since this is what my books have been about, then it is a question both about what happens when I do trust it, and exploring what interferes with that trust. Is it partly wanting to do it all myself? A kind of omnipotent wilfulness that wants to be in total control. Also, especially, an inability to trust my body. Didn't I once quote "the body is a great sagacity"?

An analyst's touch

D.W. putting his hand on my bare left shoulder. That's all the dream said.

Free thought: This is the shoulder that was hunched from the time of my father being away after his breakdown and me being diagnosed after a school gym class as having a crooked spine. In his analysis with me I did once put out a hand and he took it and held it for a few seconds.

Note on Appendix: Last pages

These last pages are as in the manuscript left at Milner's death: Mathew Hale, who worked with her during the last eight years of her life on *Alligators*, comments:

> On the day she died I was due to work for her and arrived at the house to find that she had died an hour or so earlier sitting up in bed working on the manuscript [...]
>
> When I returned to my own home, where I hadn't been for a week, there was an answerphone message from her, that she had left the night before her death. She was excited and urged me not to be late because she had important things to tell me – and get down on paper. I will never know exactly what they were.
>
> *Bothered by Alligators* ends as she left it. At the time, I was clear that the way we find it was not the definitive conclusion that she had in mind, but re-reading it now it is clear to me that it does contain all the material that she wanted to make the ending of. Perhaps there is an appropriateness to that; its unfinishable state. Not everything was resolvable.
>
> (Personal communication from Mathew Hale,
> March 2011)

These pages contain a poem relating to a "lovely toy," a wire biplane given to Milner by Alexander Newman, Milner's colleague and friend, with whom, I understand, there had been some disagreement.

The reference to the "Joy and Woe" poem is to William Blake's lines, important to Milner throughout her work. (see for example her paper of 1947–48: "Some signposts – blackness, joy, mind."[1] The lines are:

> Man was made for Joy and Woe;
> And when this we rightly know,
> Thro' the World we safely go.

(Blake, *Auguries of Innocence*)

[1] Marion Milner, "Some signposts – blackness, joy, mind," in *The Suppressed Madness of Sane Men* [1987], Hove: Routledge, 2002, p. 63.

Appendix: Last pages

Obvi... to find ways of talking about my own
experience ... at the age ... However, books have to stop
some... with a poem that I found I had recently written, or it
had written itself.

When your lovely toy arrived

I saw it

As if each of my middle fingers

Had a light on its tip

like a glow worm has

Only I think it has it on its bottom

And I was dancing in a totally dark place

With the light on my finger tips leaving a glowing trail

Like the white trail across the sky that an airoplane sometimes leaves

And then I saw it was an airoplane that you sent

For months I have not found a word for the shape my weaving lights make

But this morning, at 6 a.m. I knew it was like the cocoon a silkworm makes

Out of which something quite different may emerge

My own first thought, bareing in mind tthe "Chumps" picture, was that the word

"Chump" half rhymes with "munch" and that the catapiller bit of me (J's Pillow cat?)

has needed to spin a cocoon within which new ways of being can grow. Rather like the space time cocoon of the analytic session.

[This is not the complete conclusion. M.M. intends to add the Joy and Woe poem by William Blake here.]